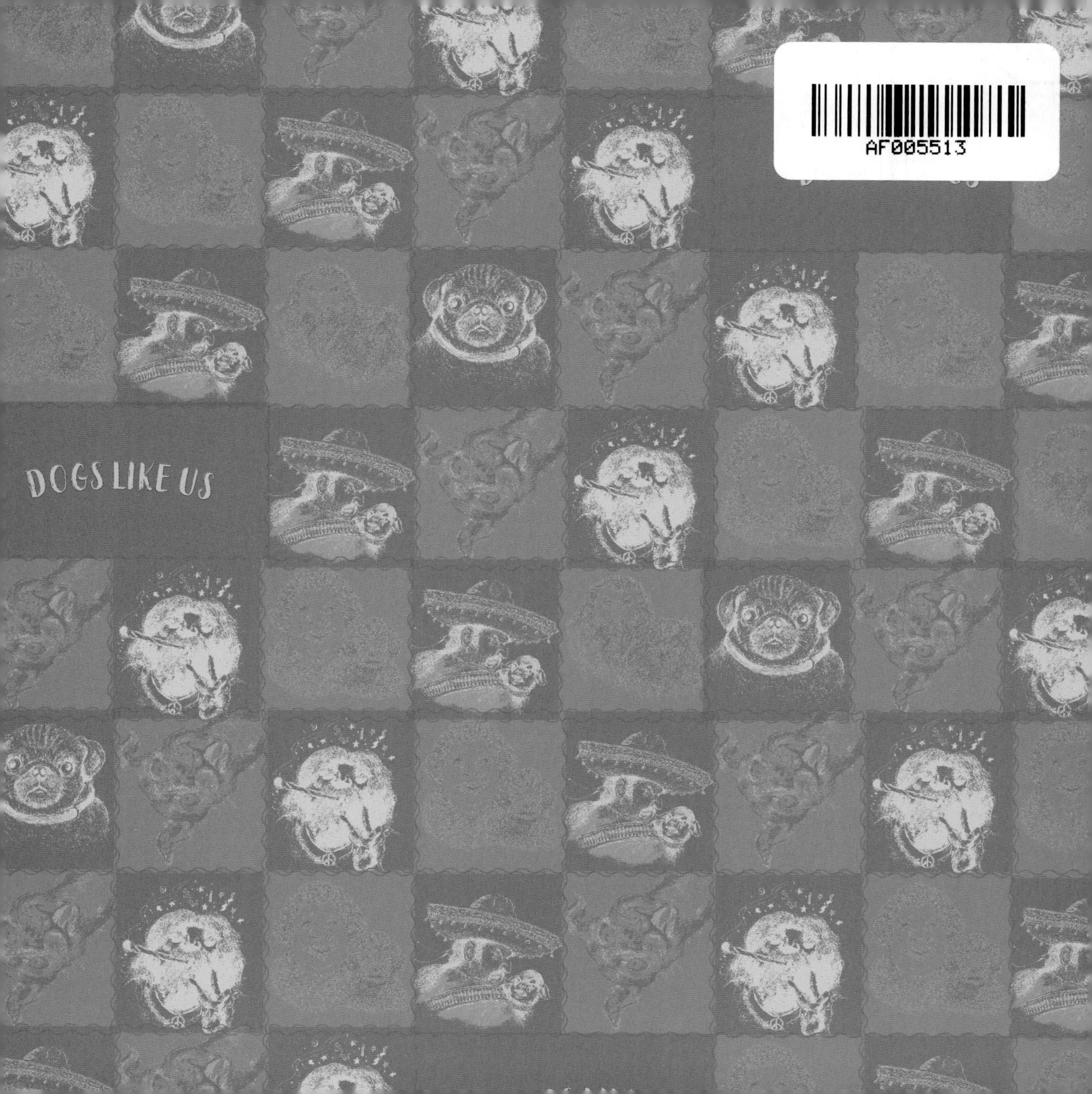
DOGS LIKE US

DOGS LIKE US

Also by John Holder

No Dogs on the Bed

Copyright © 2023 John Holder

First published in the UK in 2023 by Quiller, an imprint of Amberley Publishing Ltd.

British Library Cataloguing-in-Publication Data
A catalogue record for this book is available from the British Library.

ISBN 978 1 84689 384 1 (hardback)
ISBN 978 1 84689 385 8 (e-book)

The right of John Holder to be identified as the author of this work has been asserted in accordance with the Copyright, Design and Patent Act 1988.

The information in this book is true and complete to the best of our knowledge. All recommendations are made without any guarantee on the part of the Publisher, who also disclaims any liability incurred in connection with the use of this data or specific details.

All rights reserved. No part of this book may be reproduced or transmitted in any form or by any means, electronic or mechanical including photocopying, recording or by any information storage and retrieval system, without permission from the Publisher in writing.

Design by Becky Bowyer

Printed in China

Quiller
An imprint of Amberley Publishing Ltd

The Hill
Merrywalks
Stroud GL5 4EP
Tel: 01453 847800

Email: info@quillerbooks.com
Website: www.quillerpublishing.com

DOGS LIKE US

JOHN HOLDER

For my wife Gaye, who doesn't look anything like her cats

PEOPLE CHOOSE A dog that often resembles themselves. Apart from what you may notice whilst walking your pooch in the park, the Japanese psychologist Sadahiko Nakajima proved it in a series of experiments. Women with hair covering their ears might choose a Cavalier King Charles spaniel or a dachshund, whilst short-haired women might go for a corgi or Yorkshire terrier. Look out for that macho man with his aggressive dog straining at the lead, or the lithe jogger running with an Afghan hound.

But our relationships with our wet-nosed, furry best friends often goes further than just physical characteristics. A gentle, quiet academic wouldn't choose a boisterous collie, nor would an energetic teenager want a basset hound. A bichon frise would not be the first choice for a Hell's Angel. Perhaps the canine 'mini-me' reveals a narcissistic tendency in all of us. Put simply, we all tend to like the familiar.

"What do dogs do on their day off?
Can't lie around – that's their job!"

George Carlin

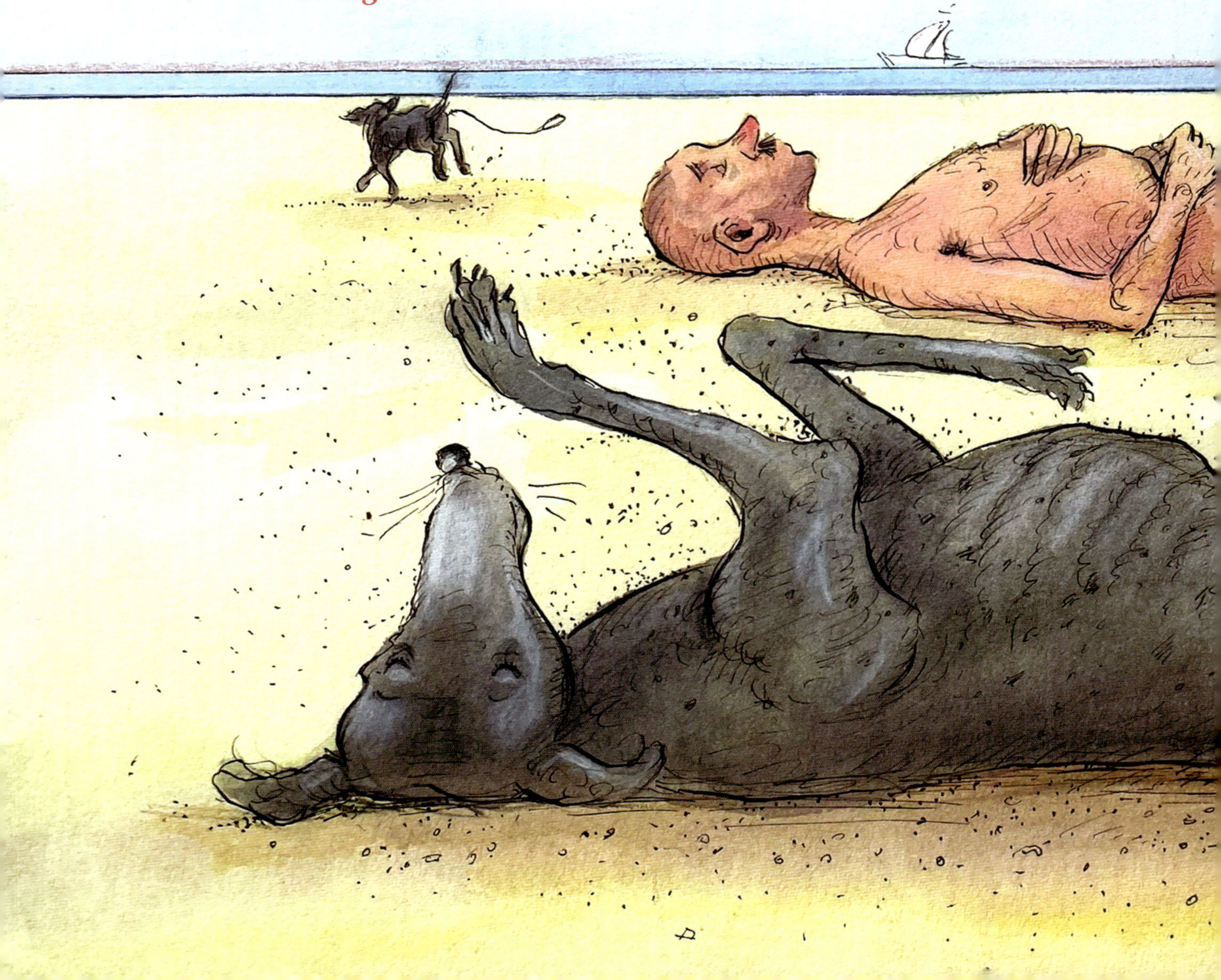

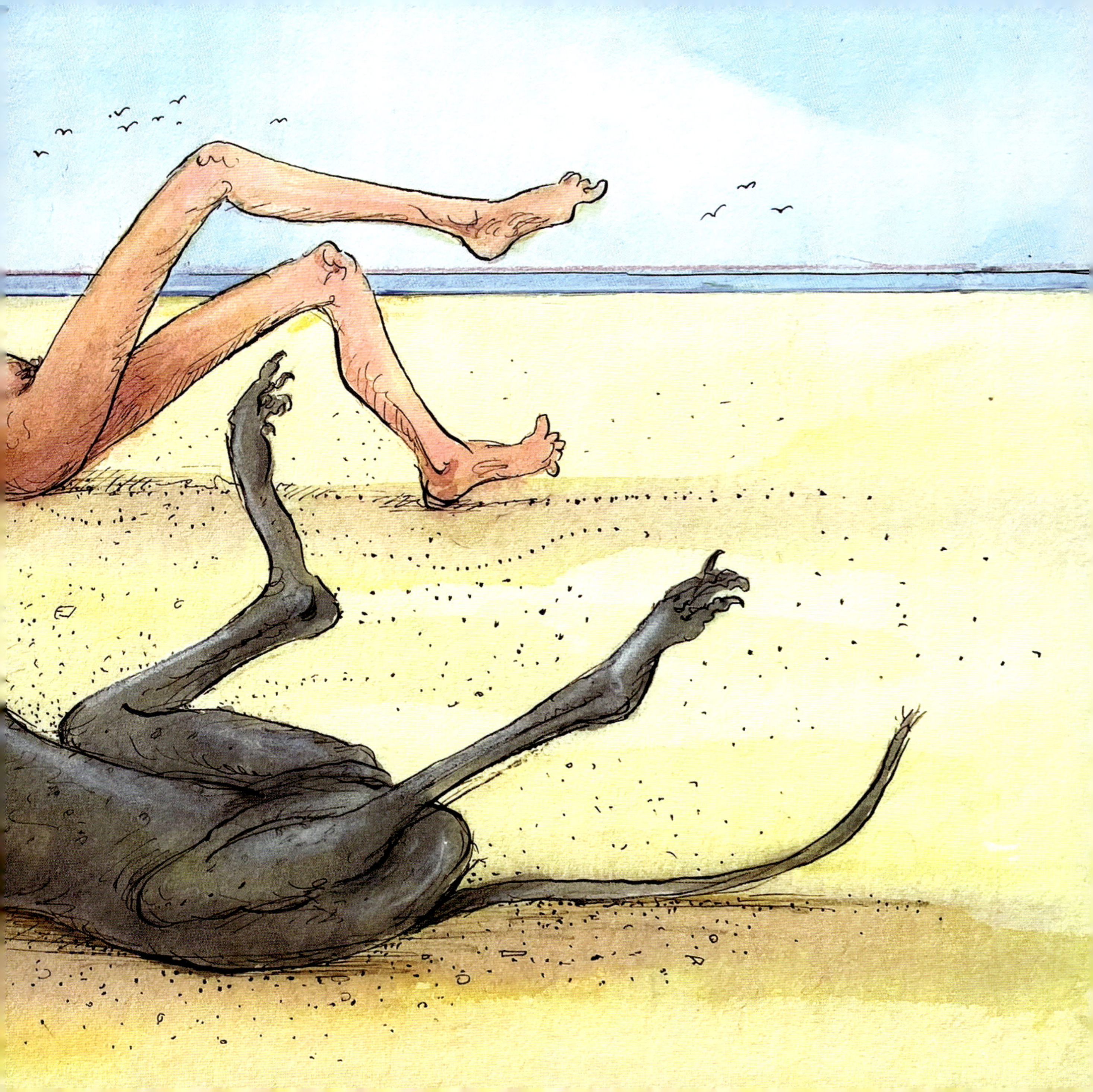

"*Every dog must have his day.*"

Jonathan Swift

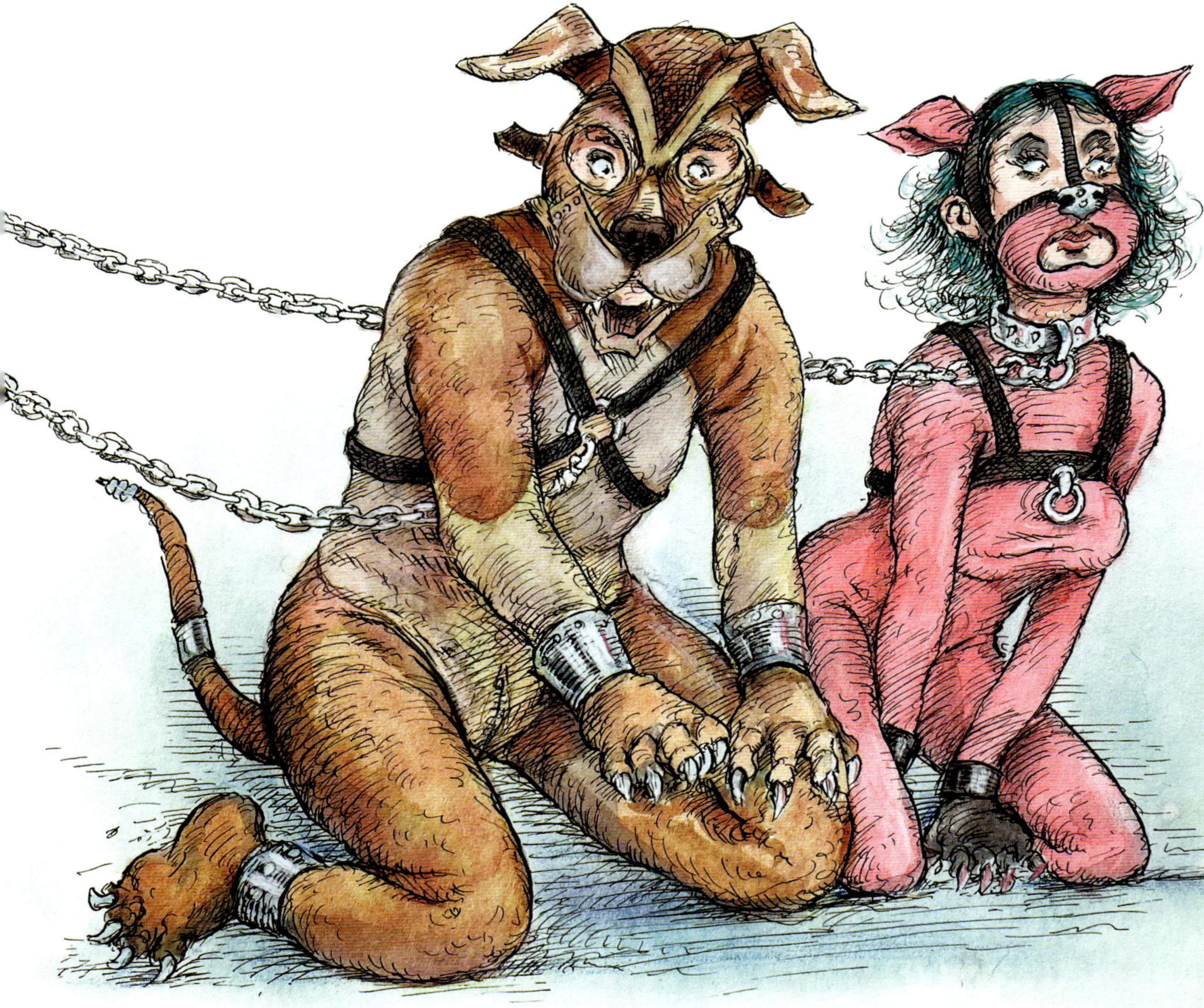

"I've seen a look in dogs' eyes, a quickly vanishing look of amazed contempt, and I am convinced that basically dogs think humans are nuts."

John Steinbeck

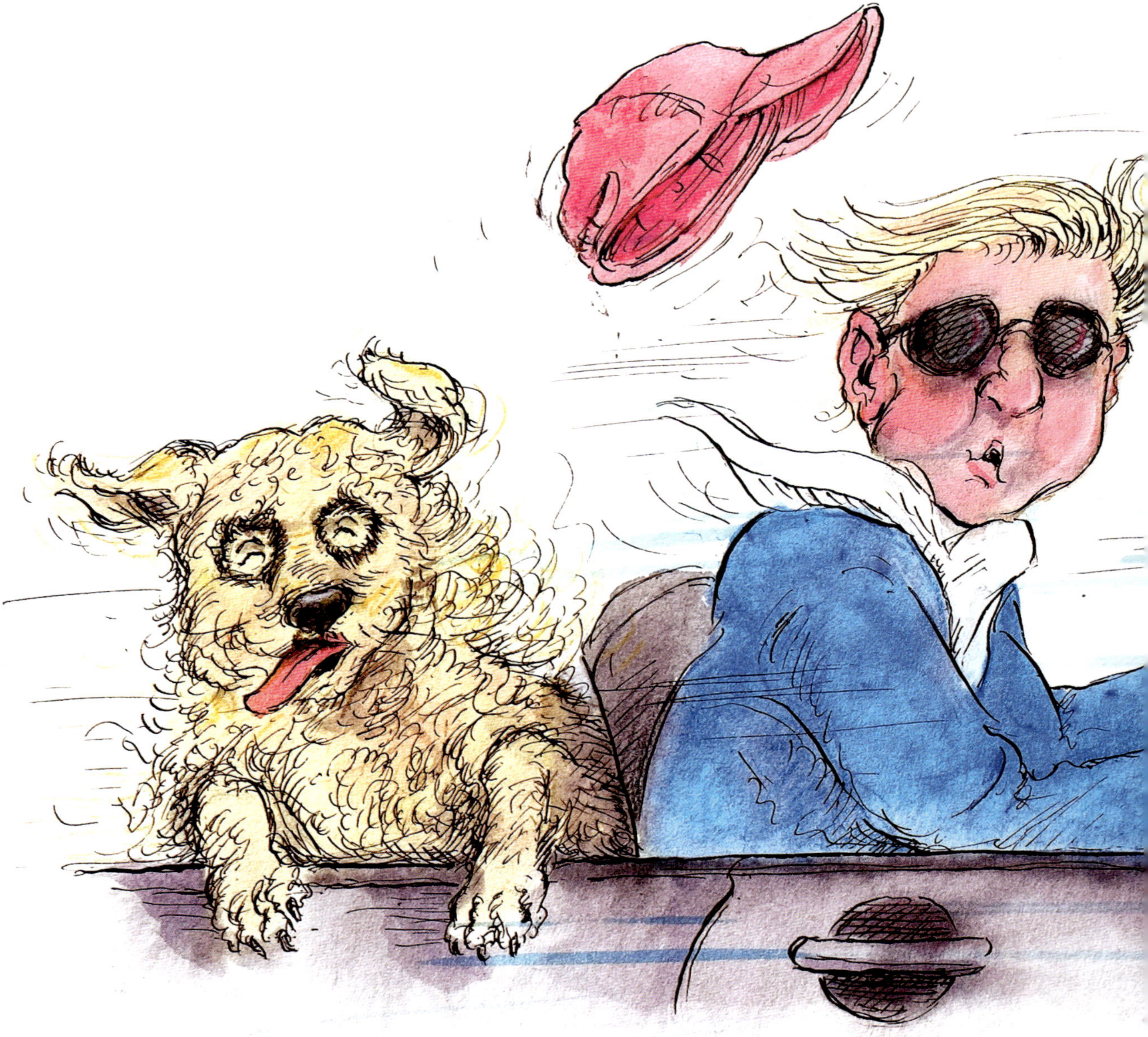

"Did you ever notice that when you blow in a dog's face he gets mad at you? But when you take him in a car he sticks his head out the window."

Steve Bluestone

"If your dog is fat you need more exercise."

Anon

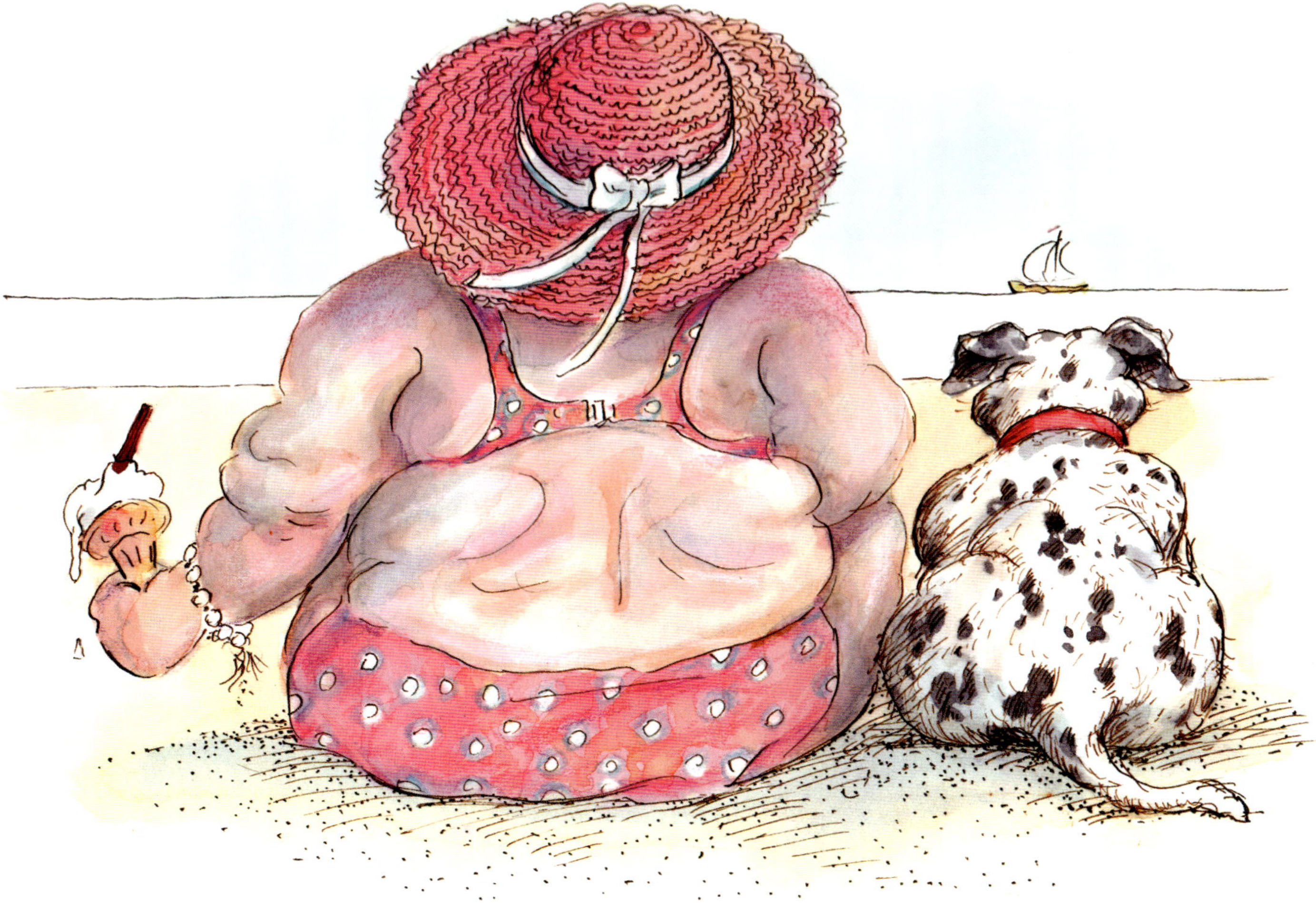

"My wife kisses the dog on the lips, yet she won't drink from my glass."

Rodney Dangerfield

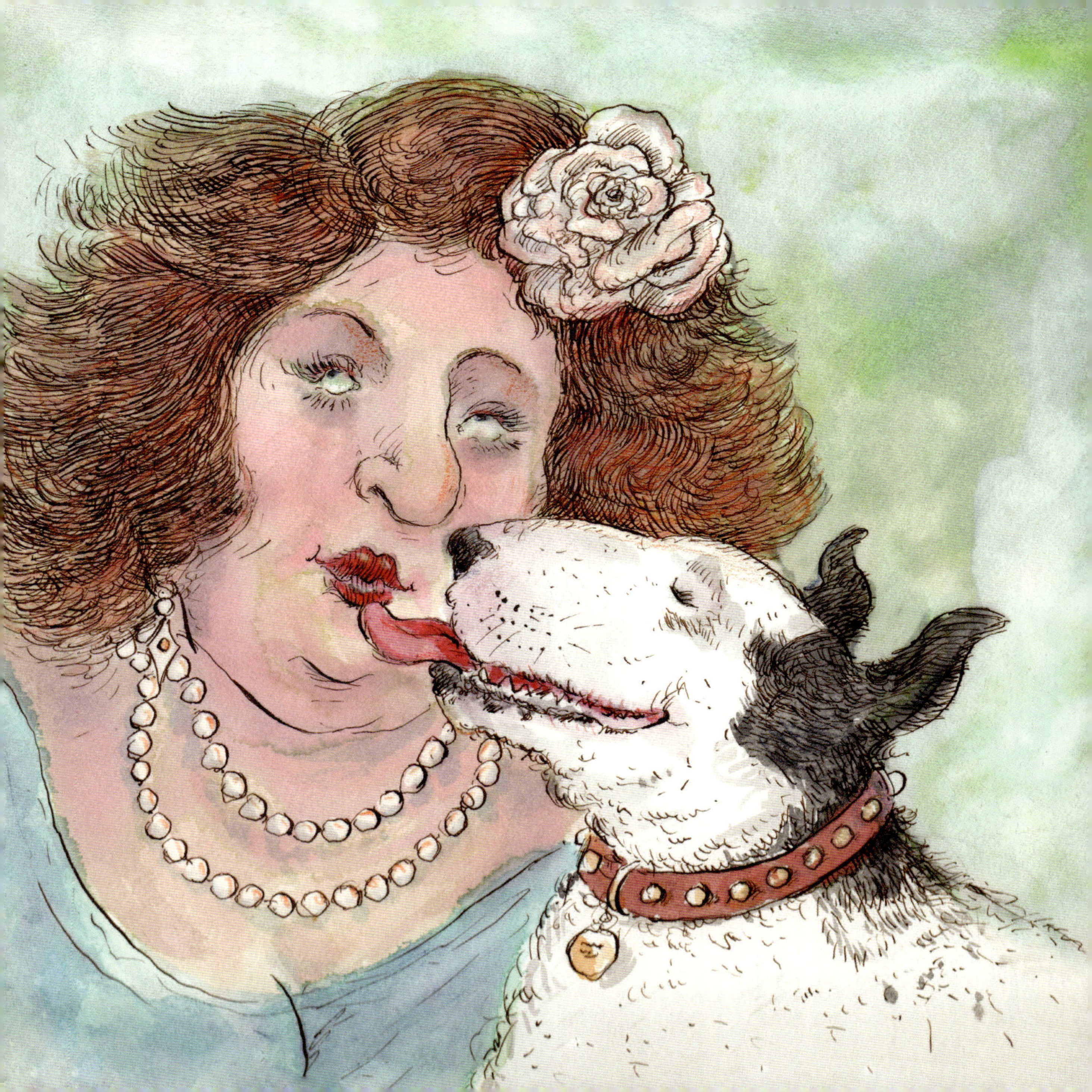

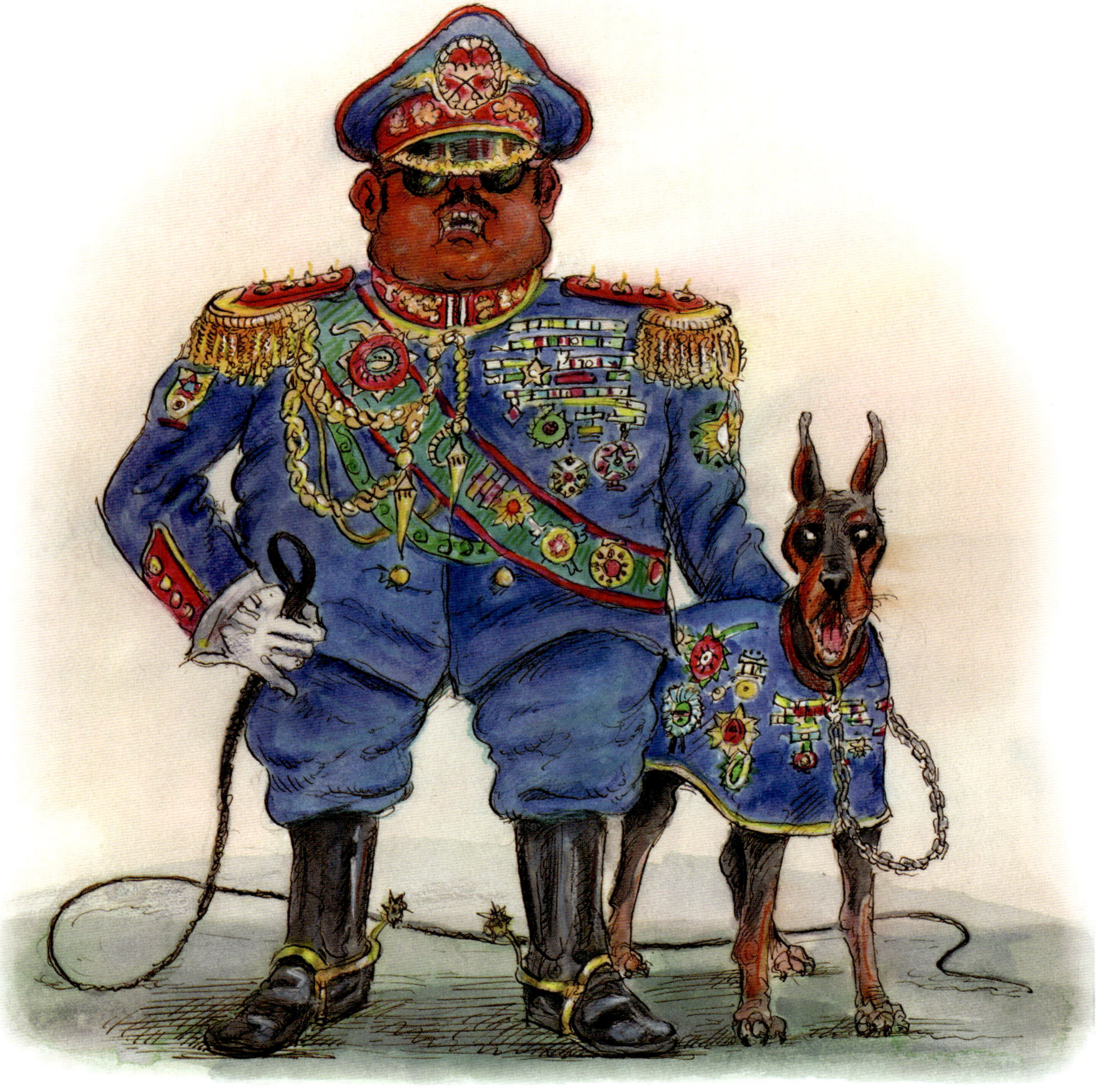

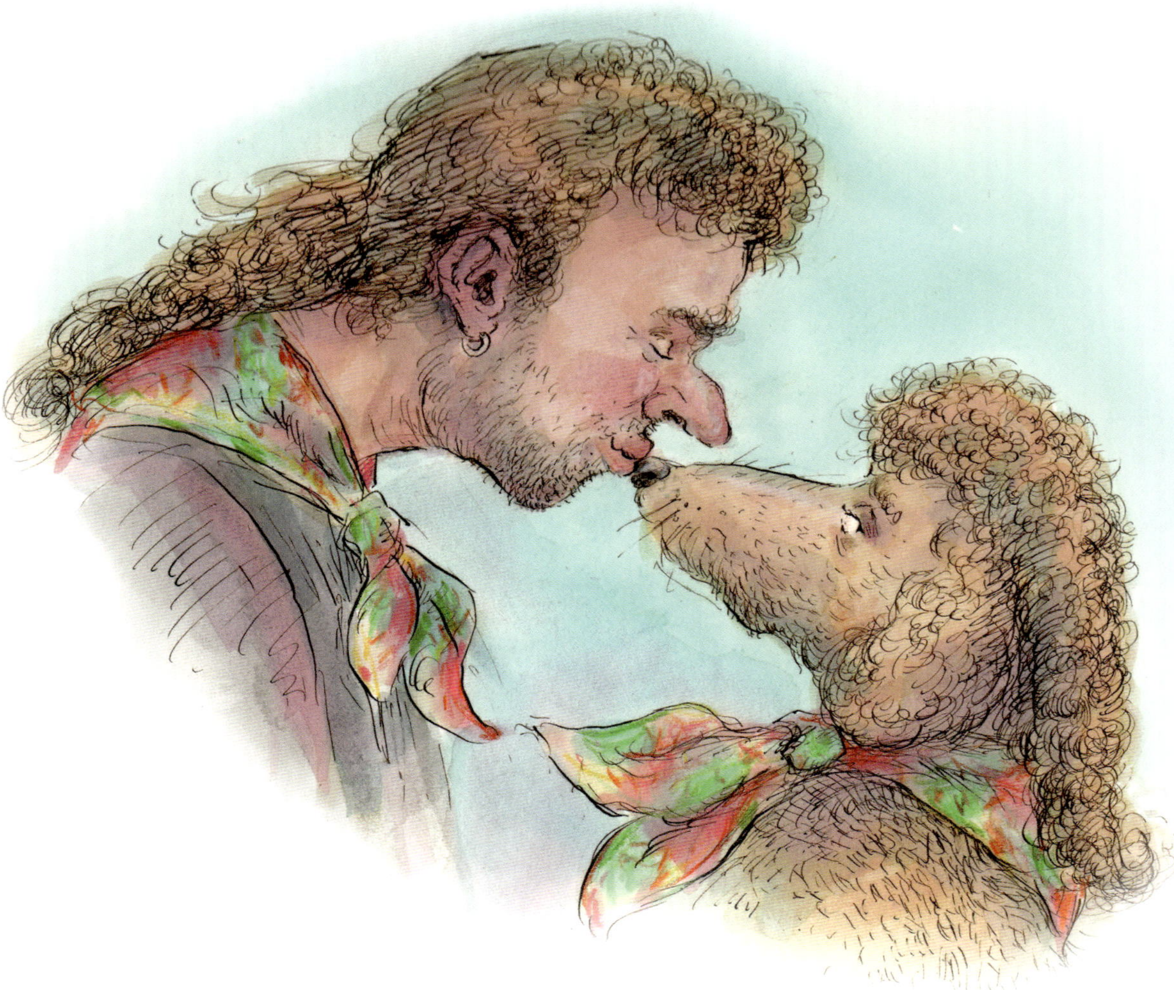

"When a man's best friend is his dog, that dog has a problem."

Edward Abbey

"Old age isn't so bad when you consider the alternative."

Maurice Chevalier

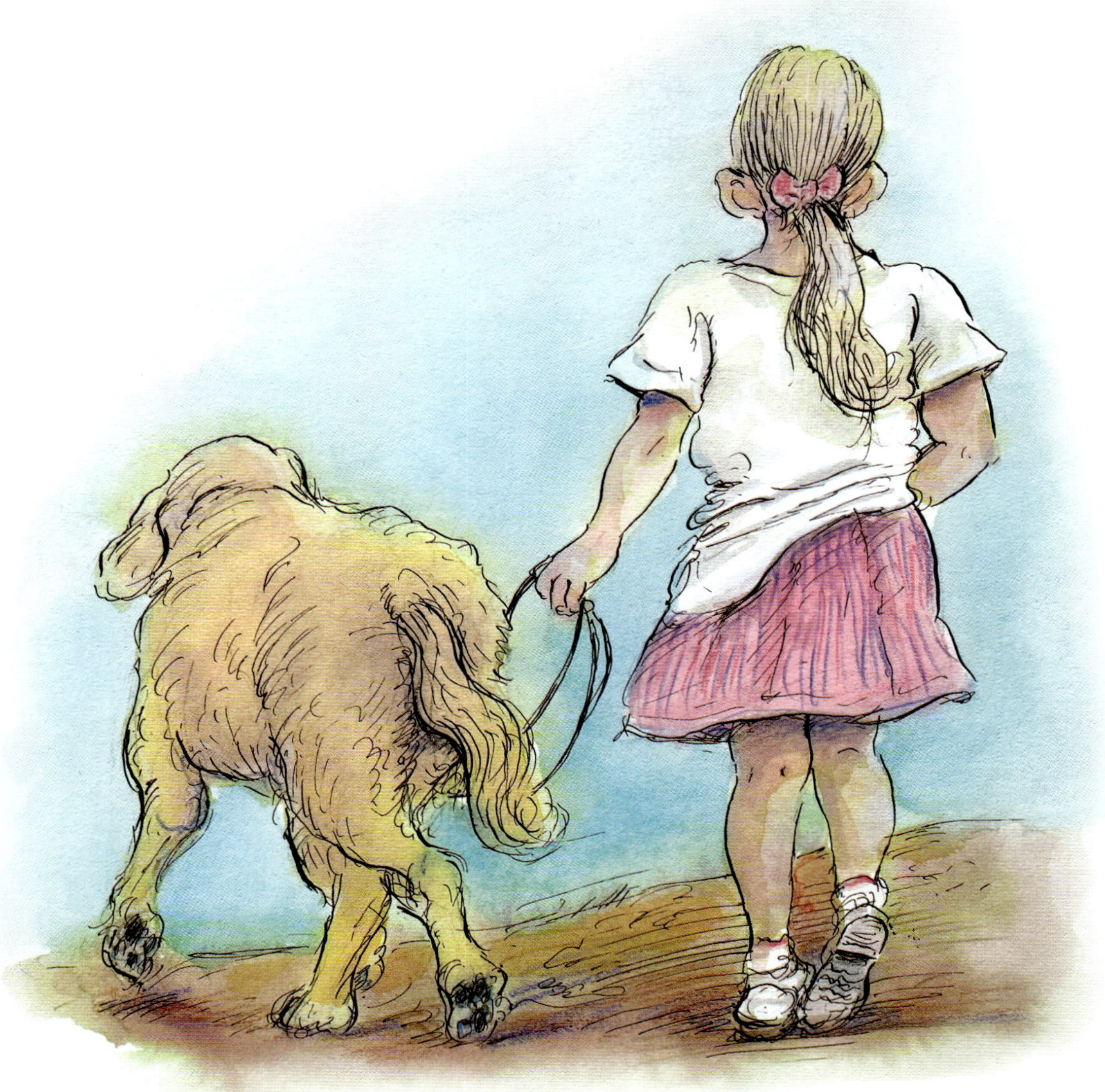

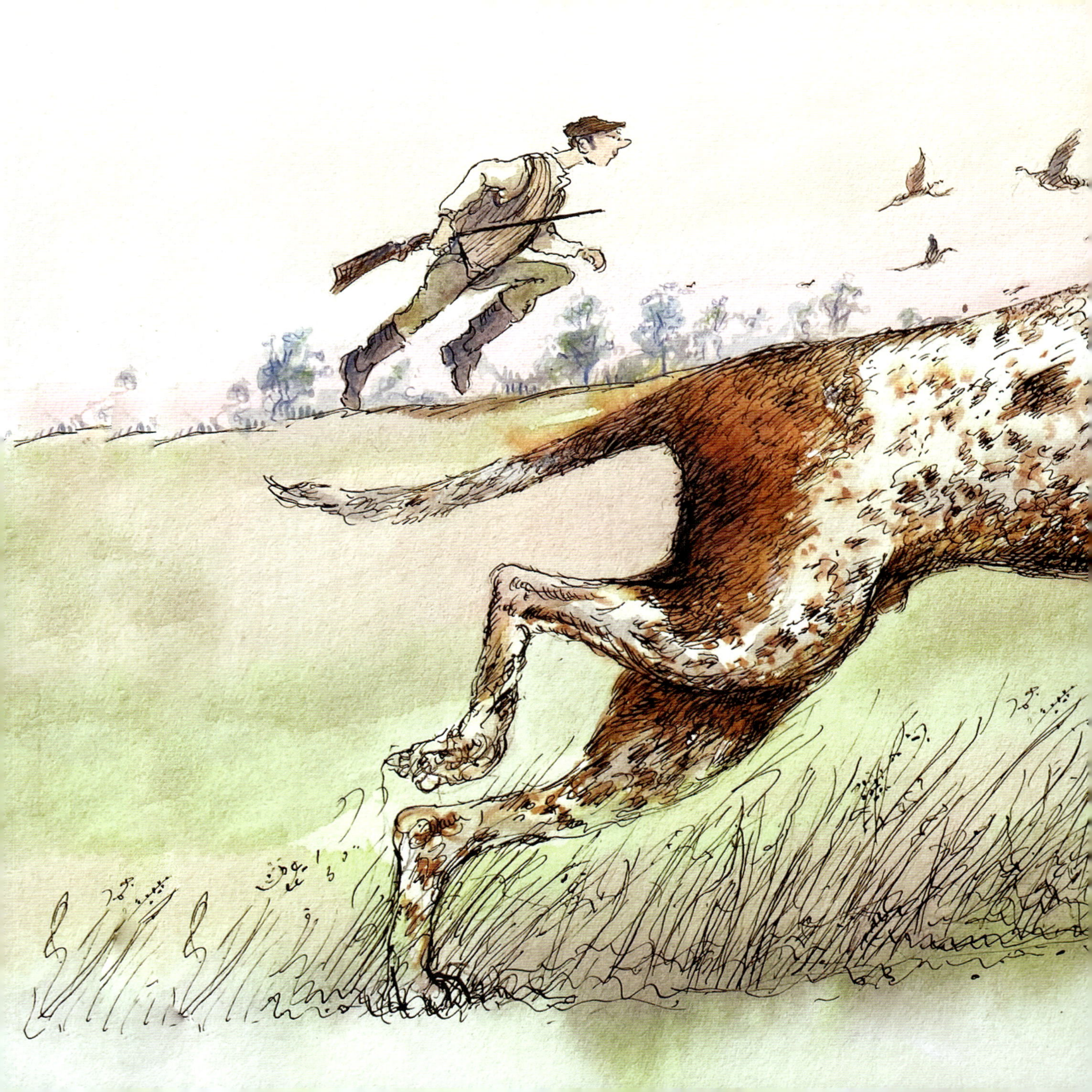

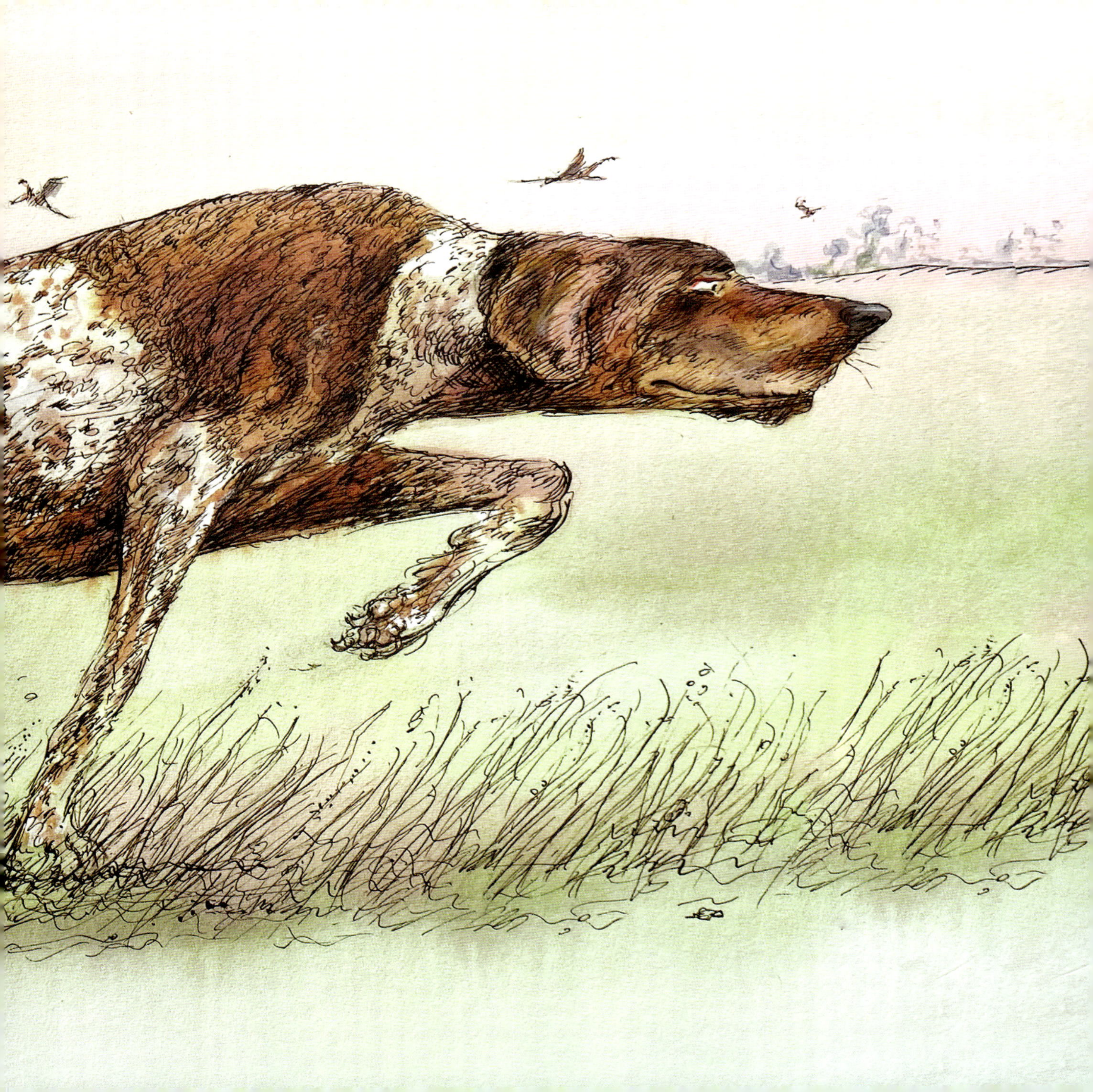

"People who wear fur smell like a wet dog if they're in the rain. And they look fat and gross."

Pamela Anderson

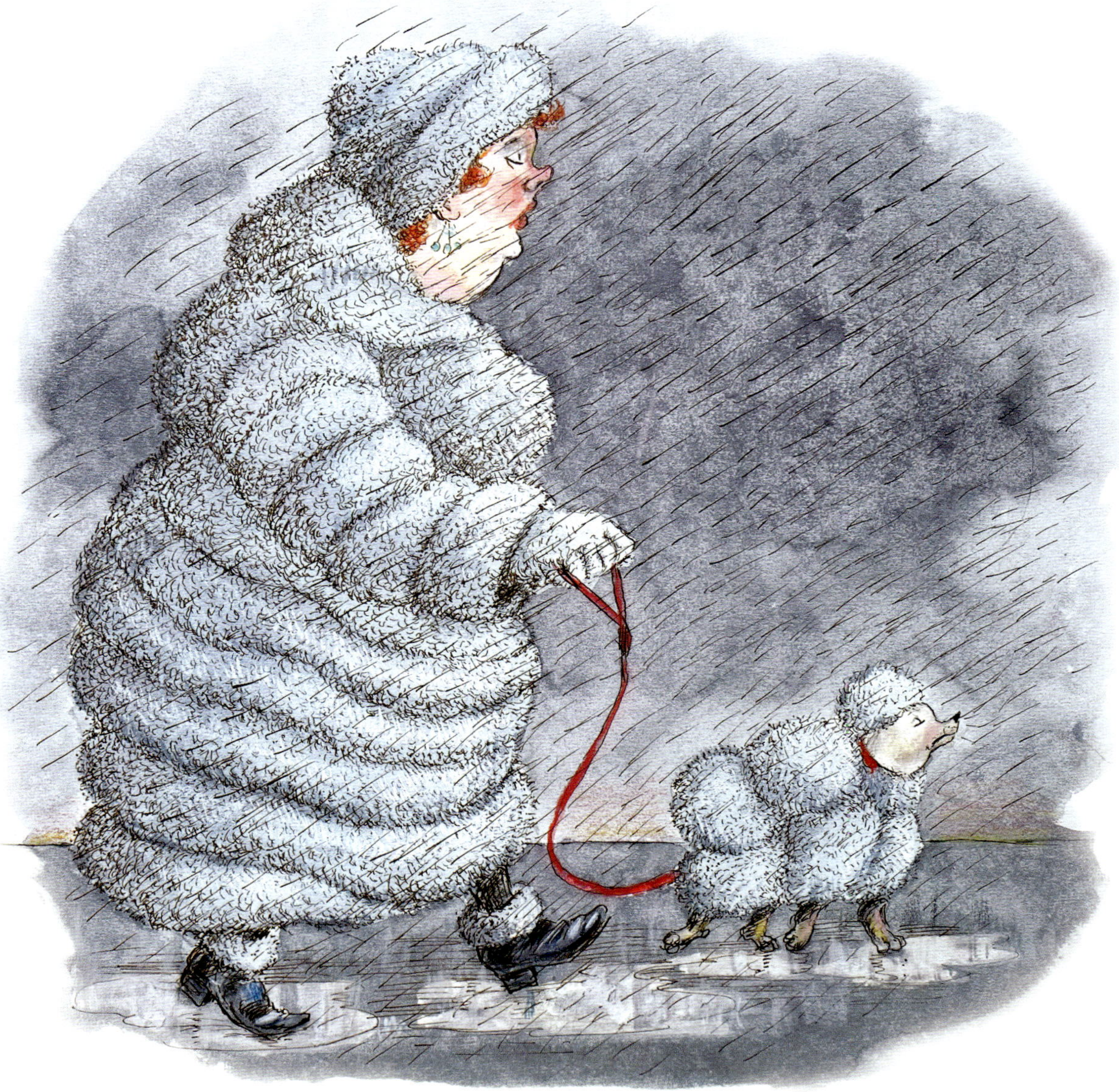

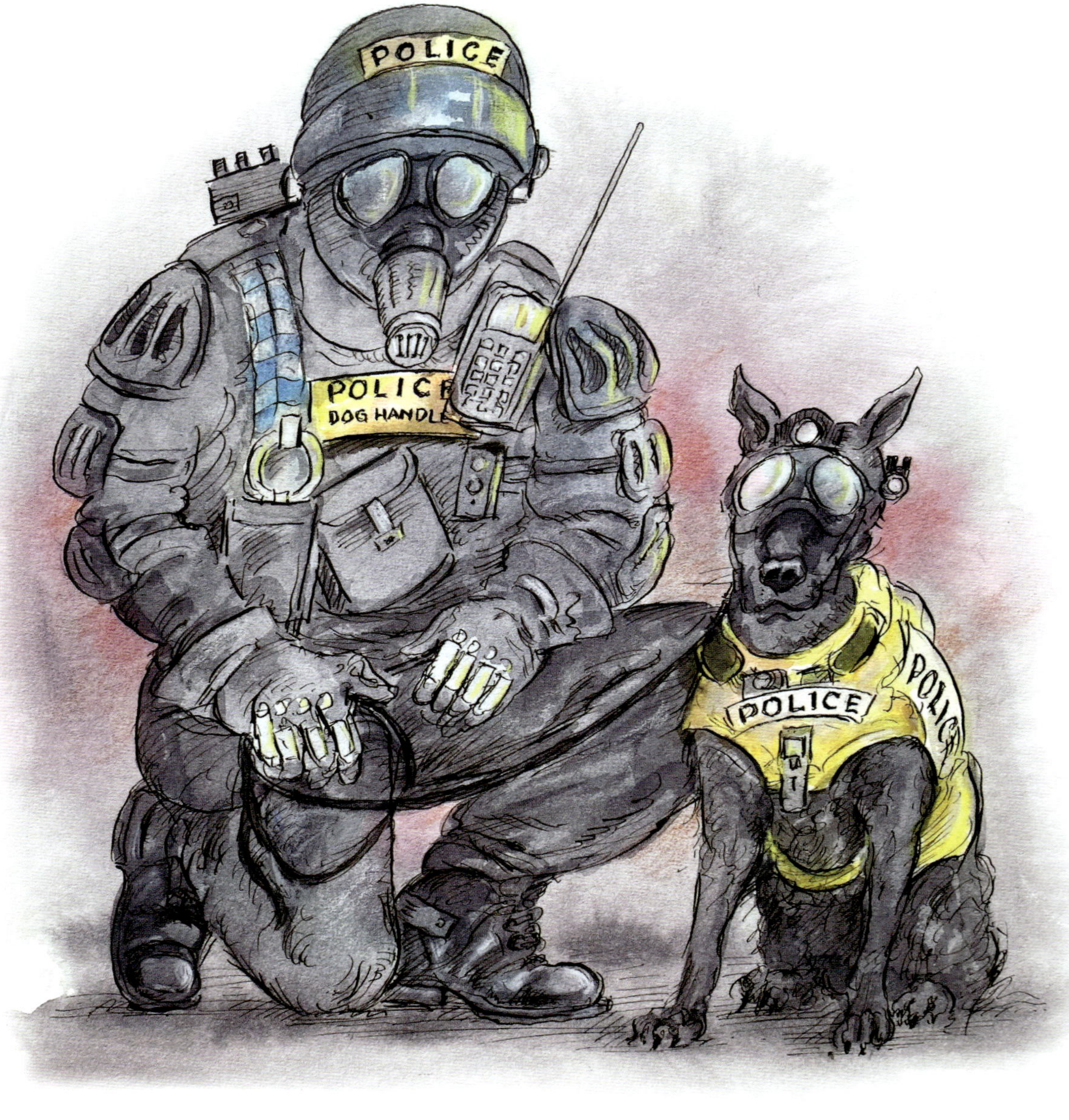
POLICE
POLICE
DOG HANDLE
POLICE
POLICE

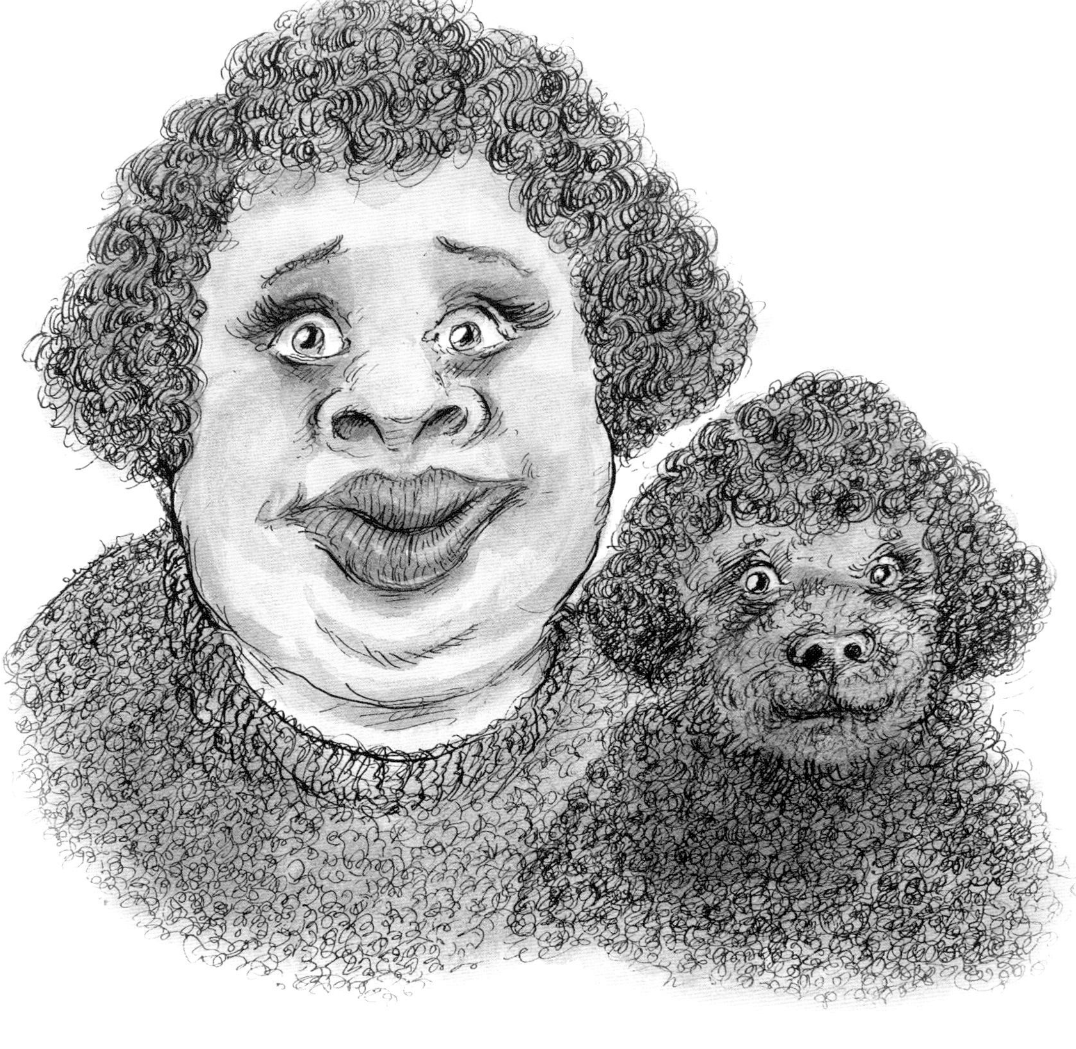

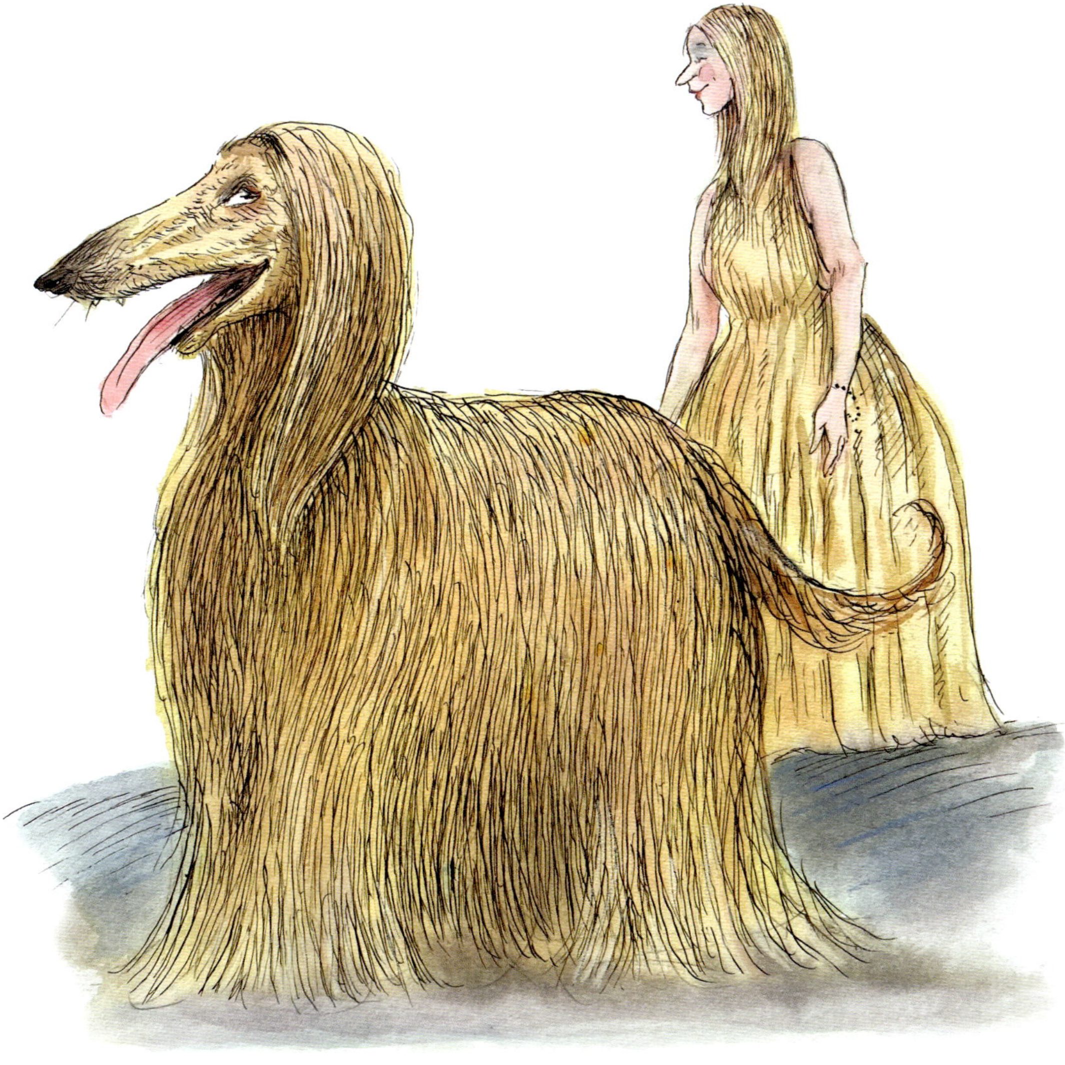

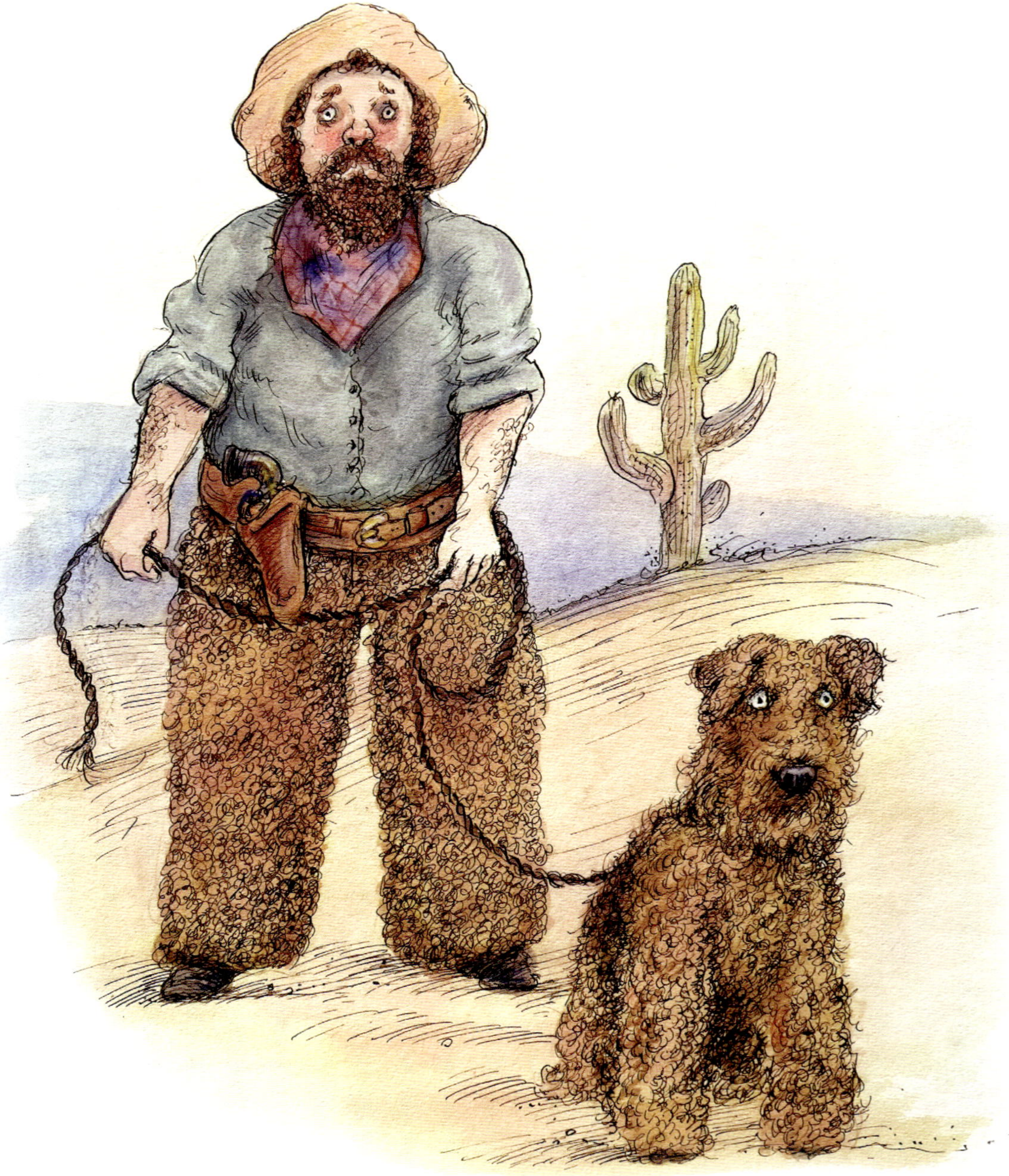

"If you don't have wrinkles, you haven't laughed enough."

Phyllis Diller

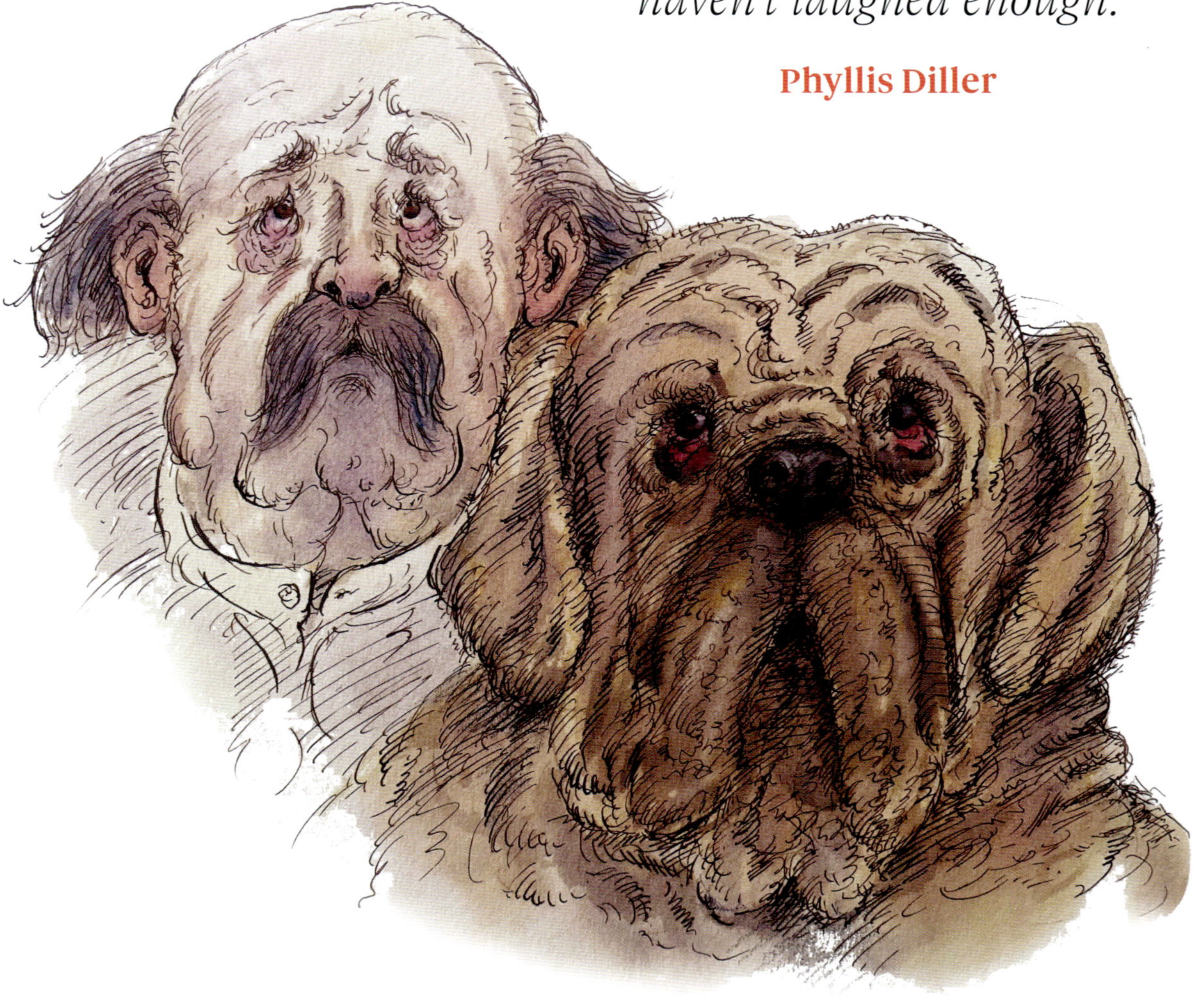

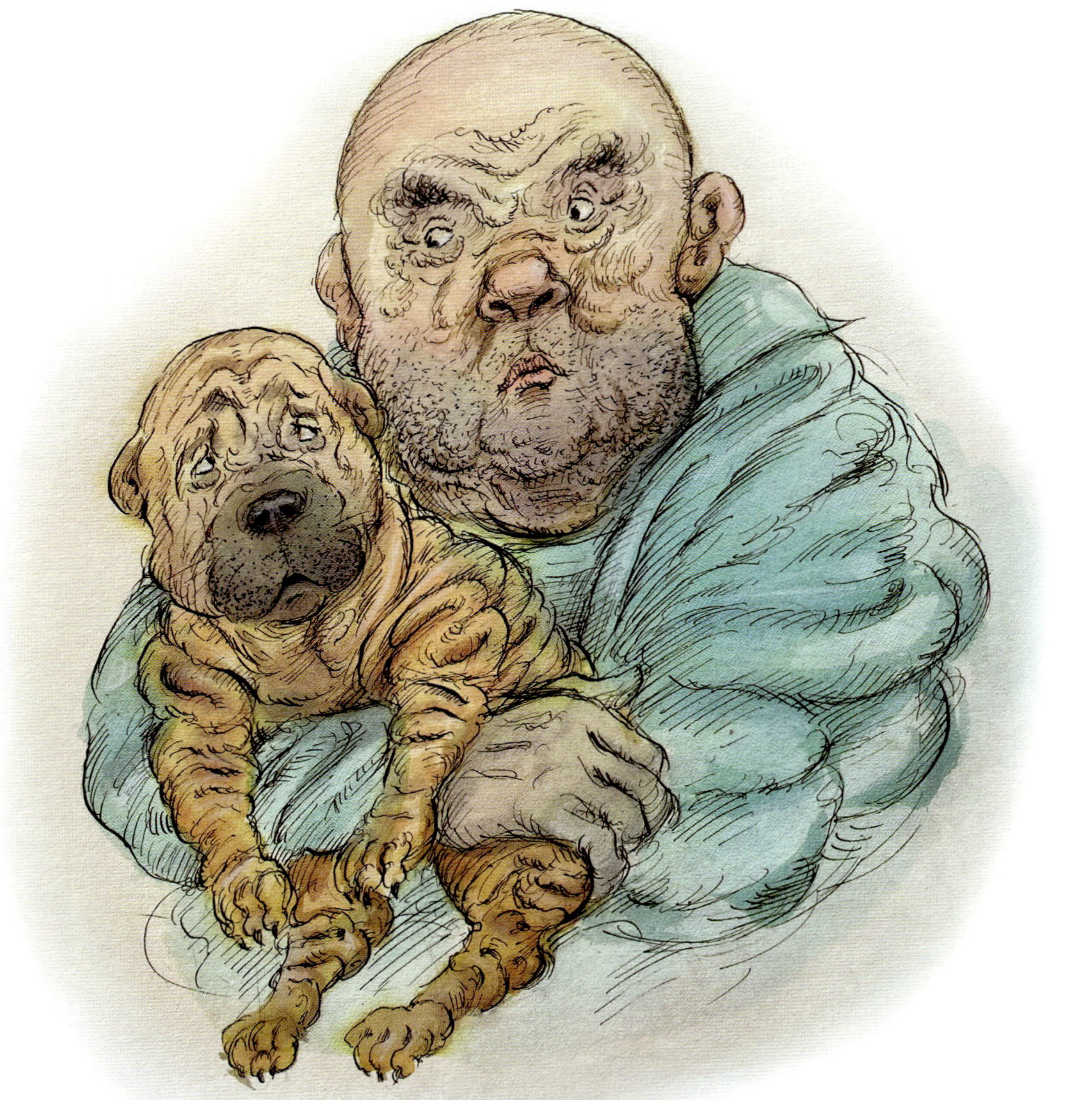

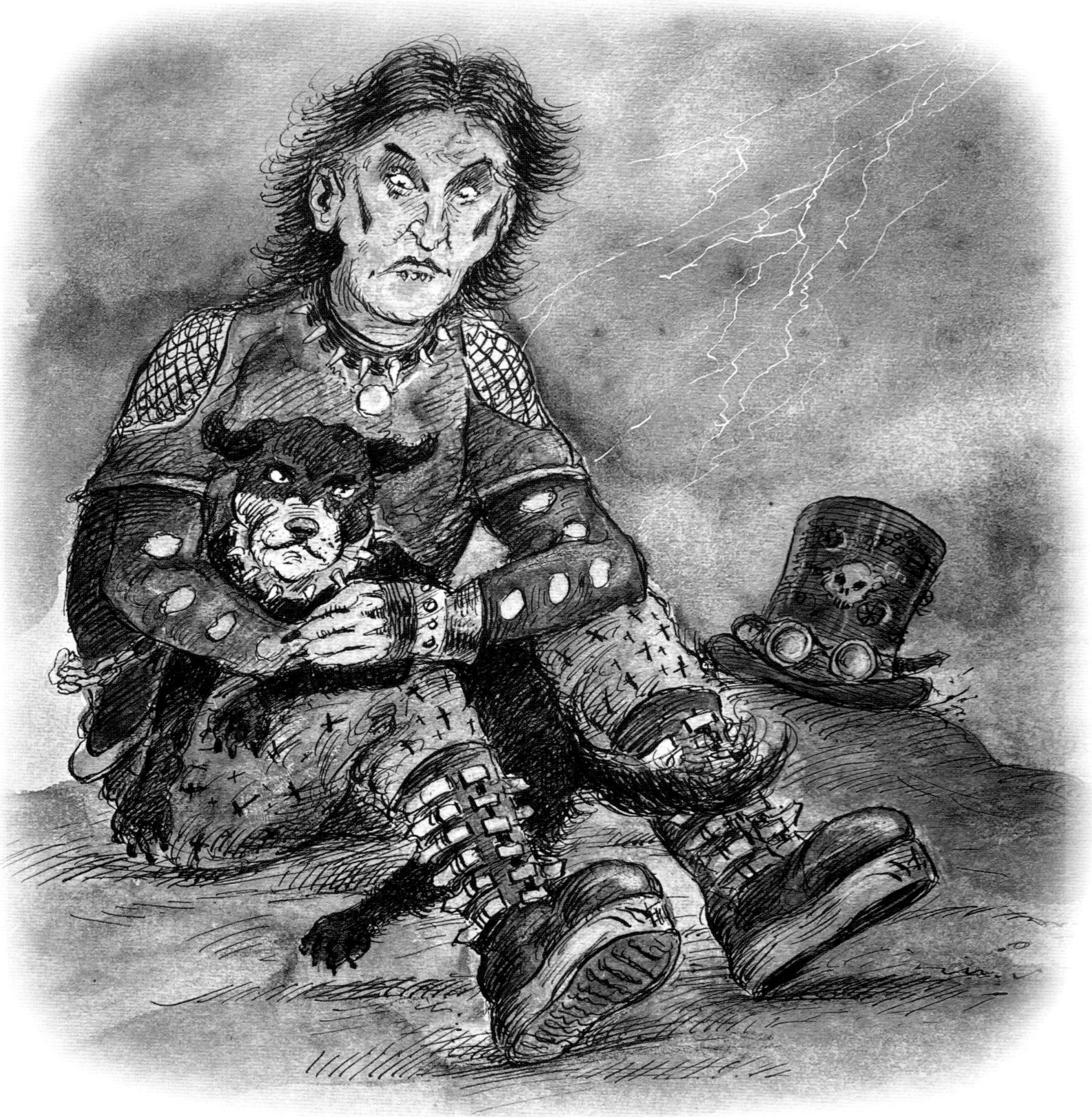

"No matter how little money and how few possessions you own, having a dog makes you rich."

Louis Sabin

"Outside of a dog, a book is man's best friend. Inside of a dog, it's too dark to read."

Groucho Marx

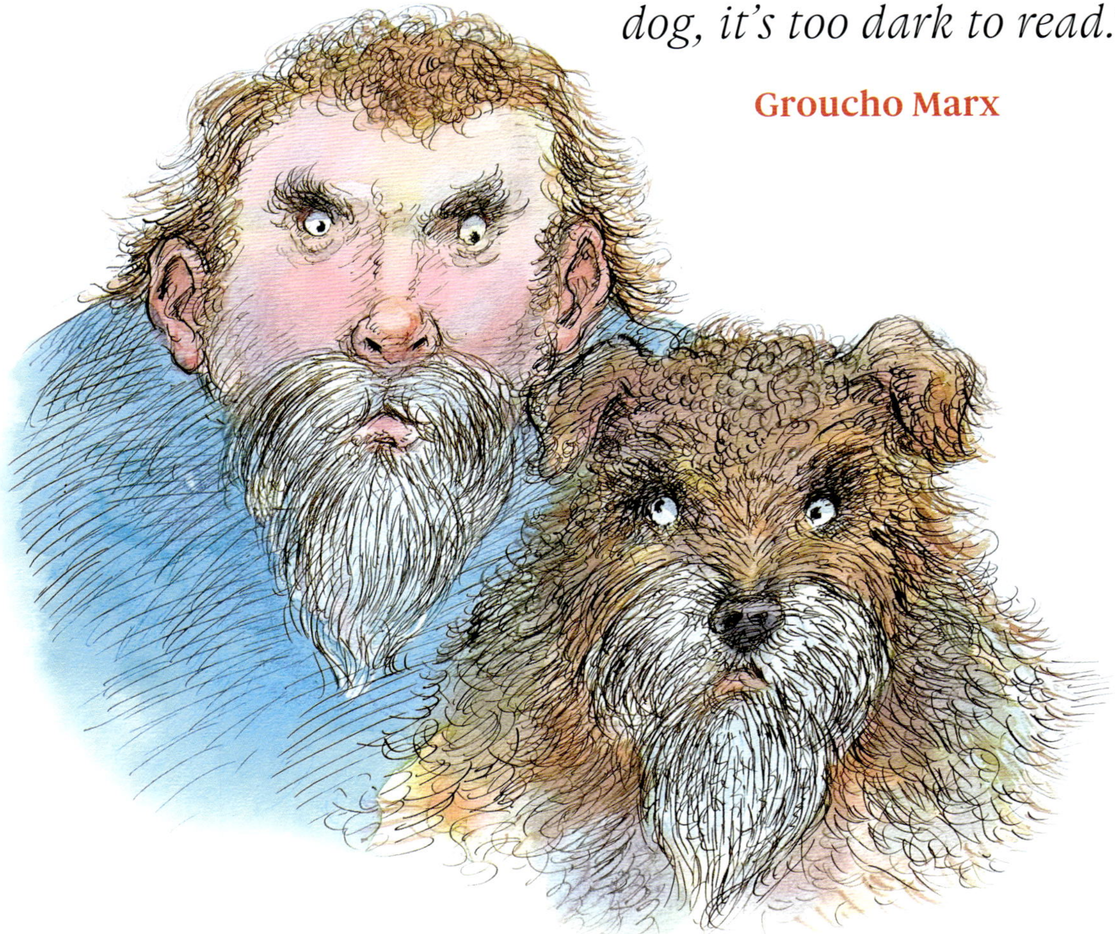

"Happiness is a warm puppy."

Charles M. Schulz

*"Even the tiniest poodle or chihuahua
is still a wolf at heart."*

Anon

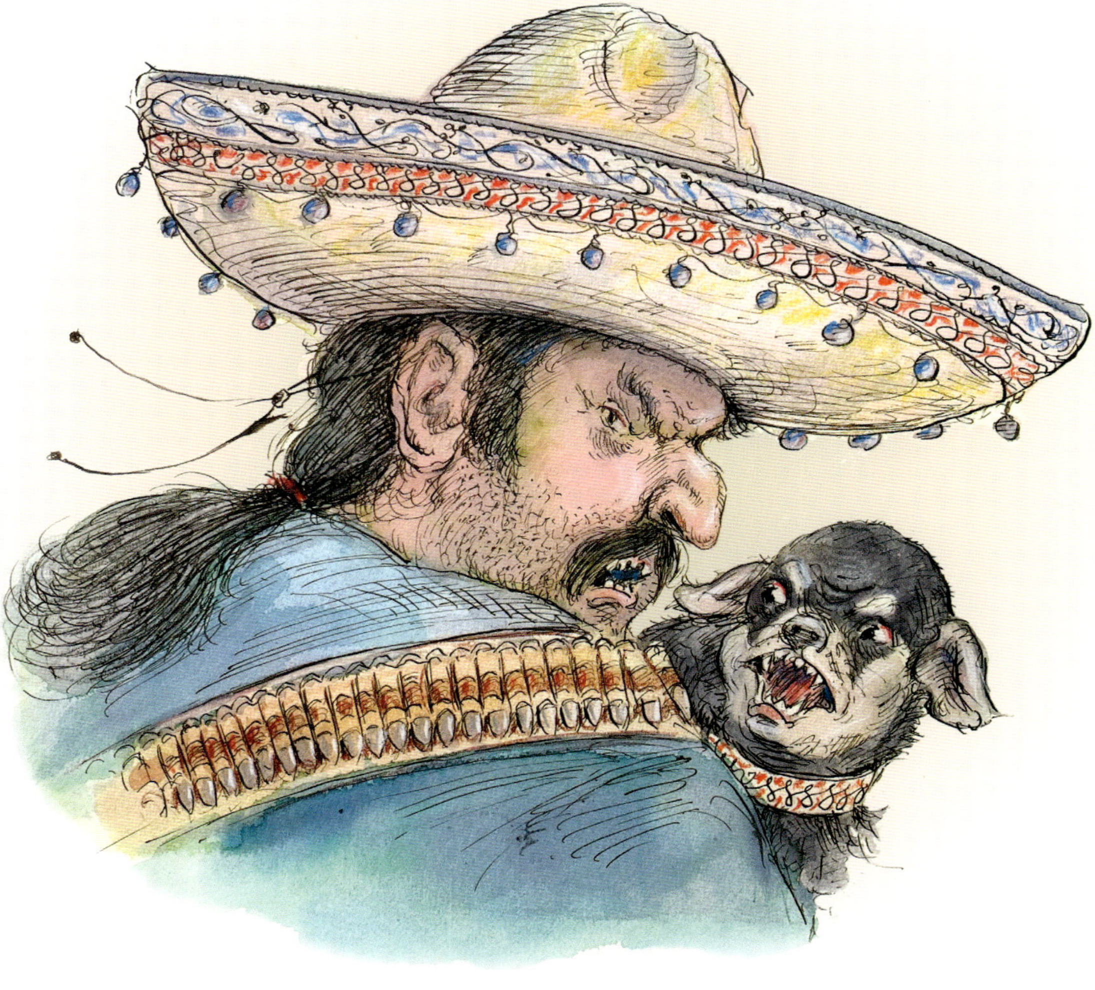

"You can usually tell that a man is good if he has a dog who loves him."

W. Bruce Cameron

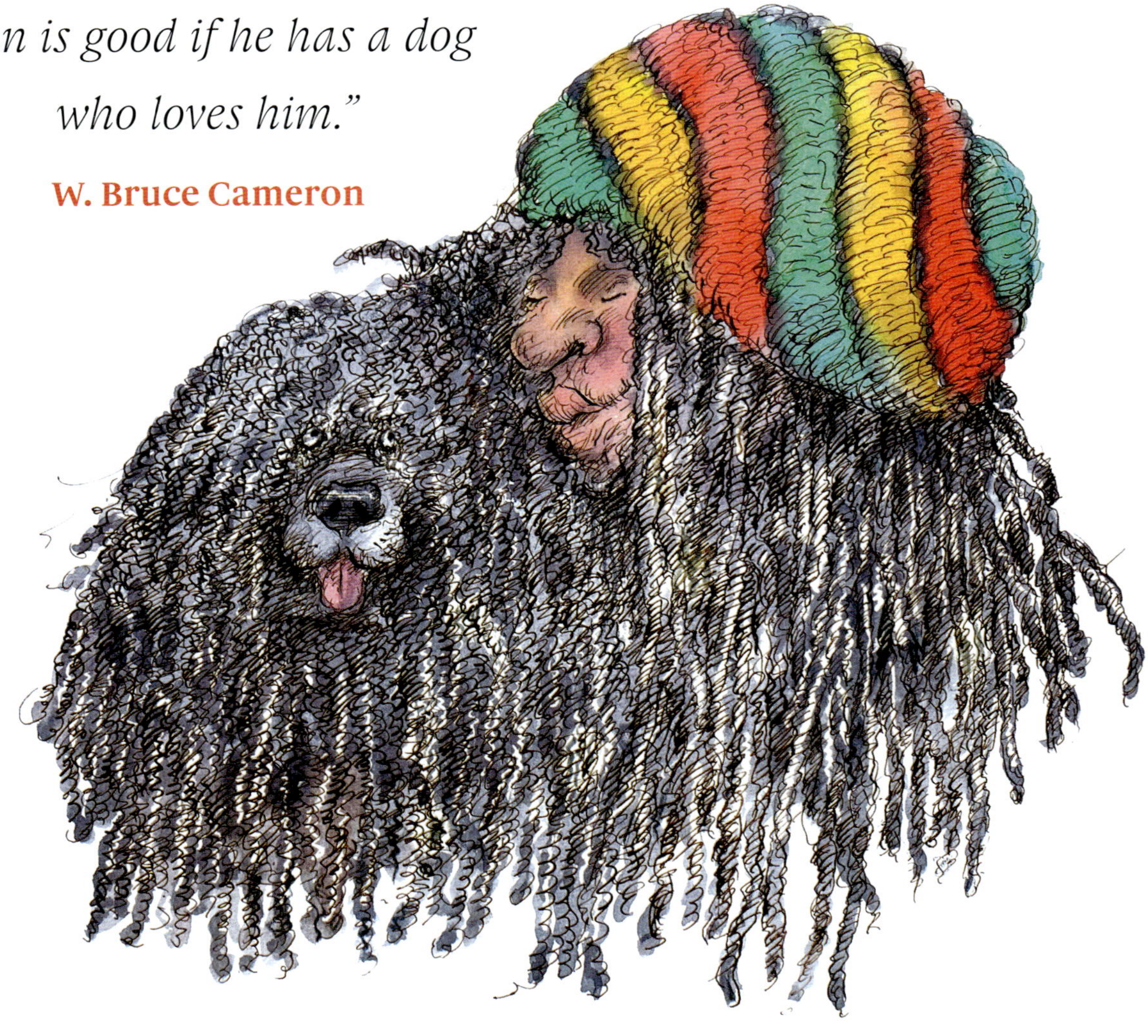

"The dog is a gentleman; I hope to go to his heaven not man's."

Mark Twain

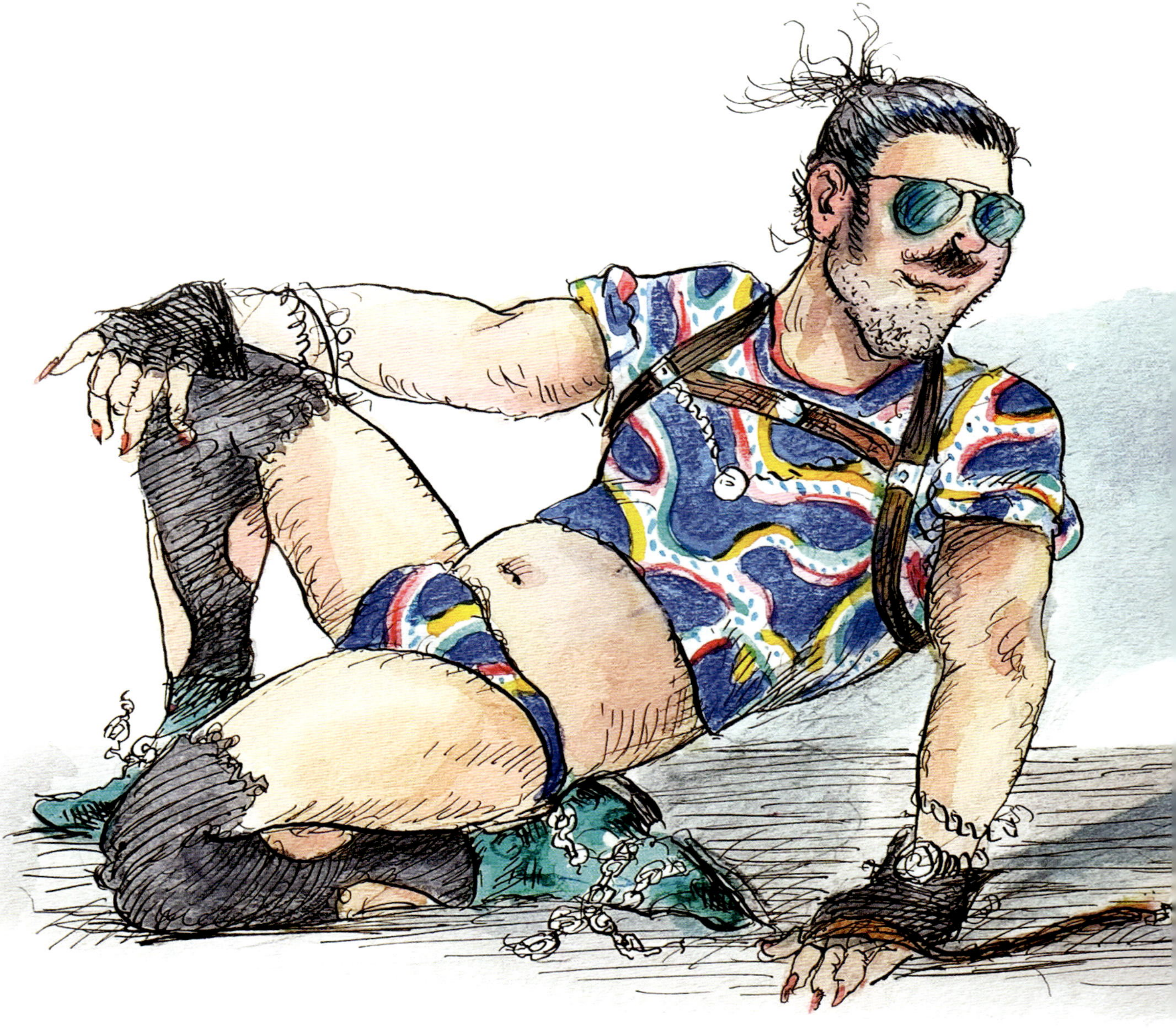

"Style is knowing who you are, what you want to say, and not giving a damn."

Orson Welles

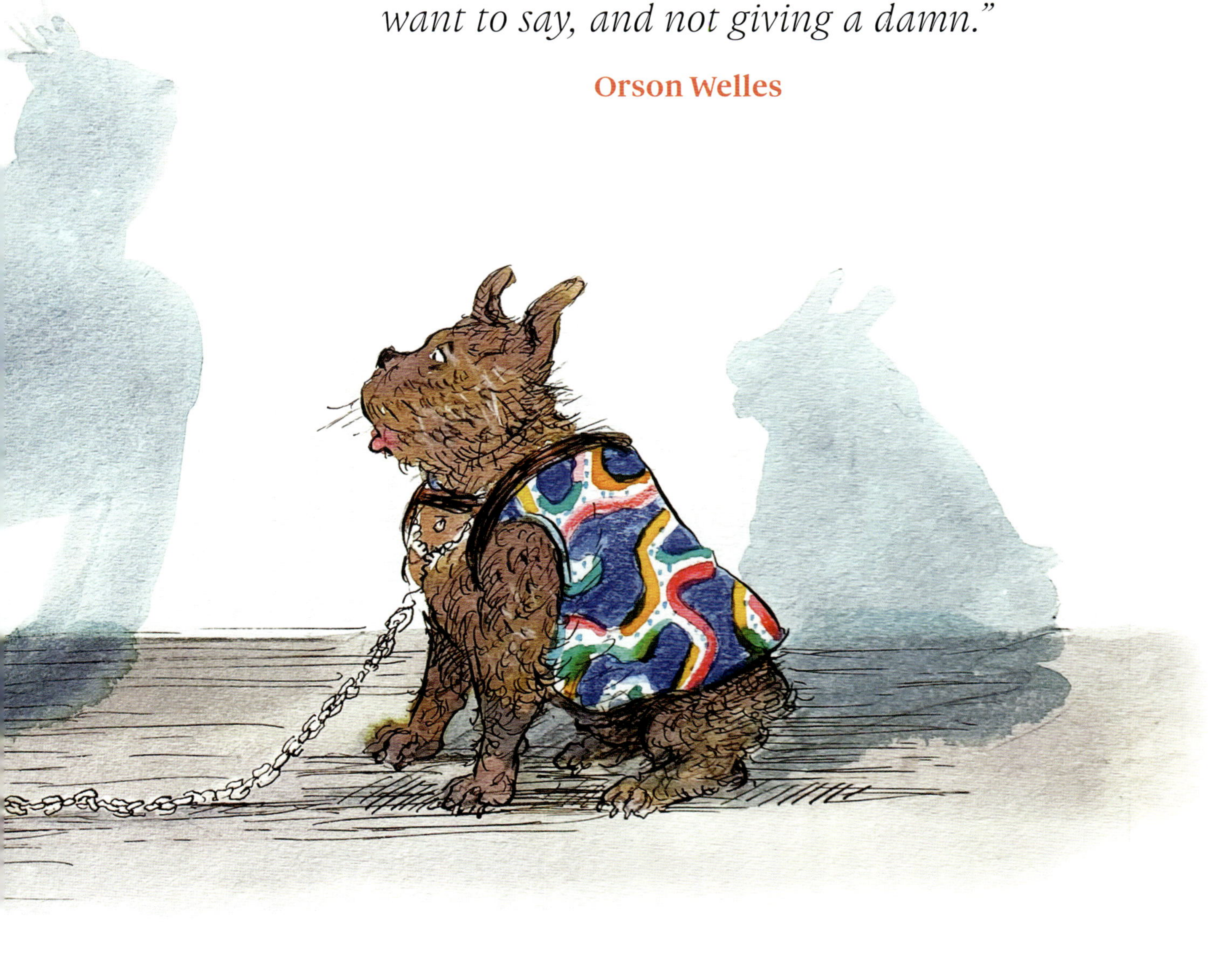

"Where words fail, music speaks."

Hans Christian Andersen

"I am your worst dream come true!"

Pennywise

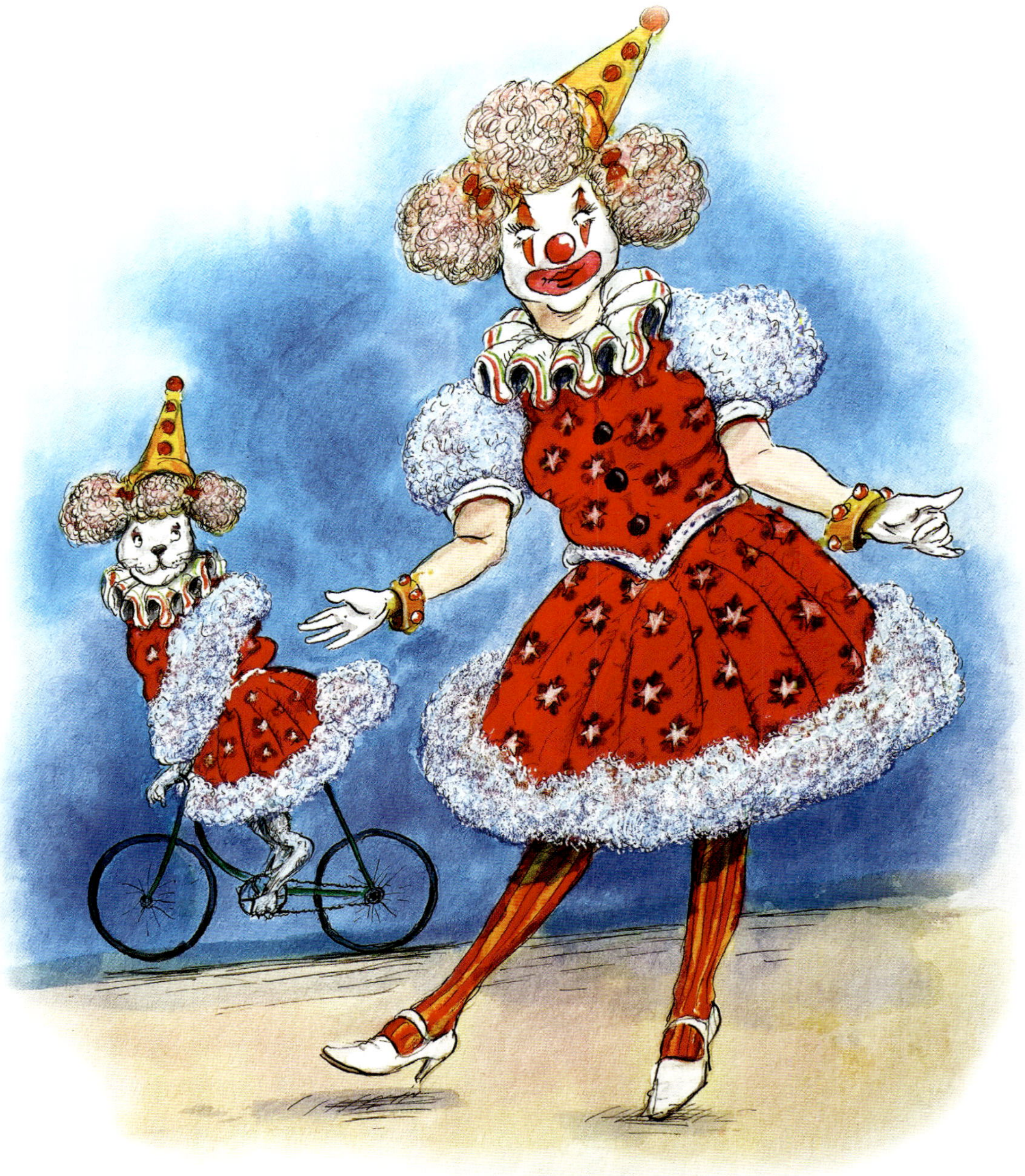

"Don't accept your dog's admiration as conclusive evidence that you are wonderful."

Ann Landers

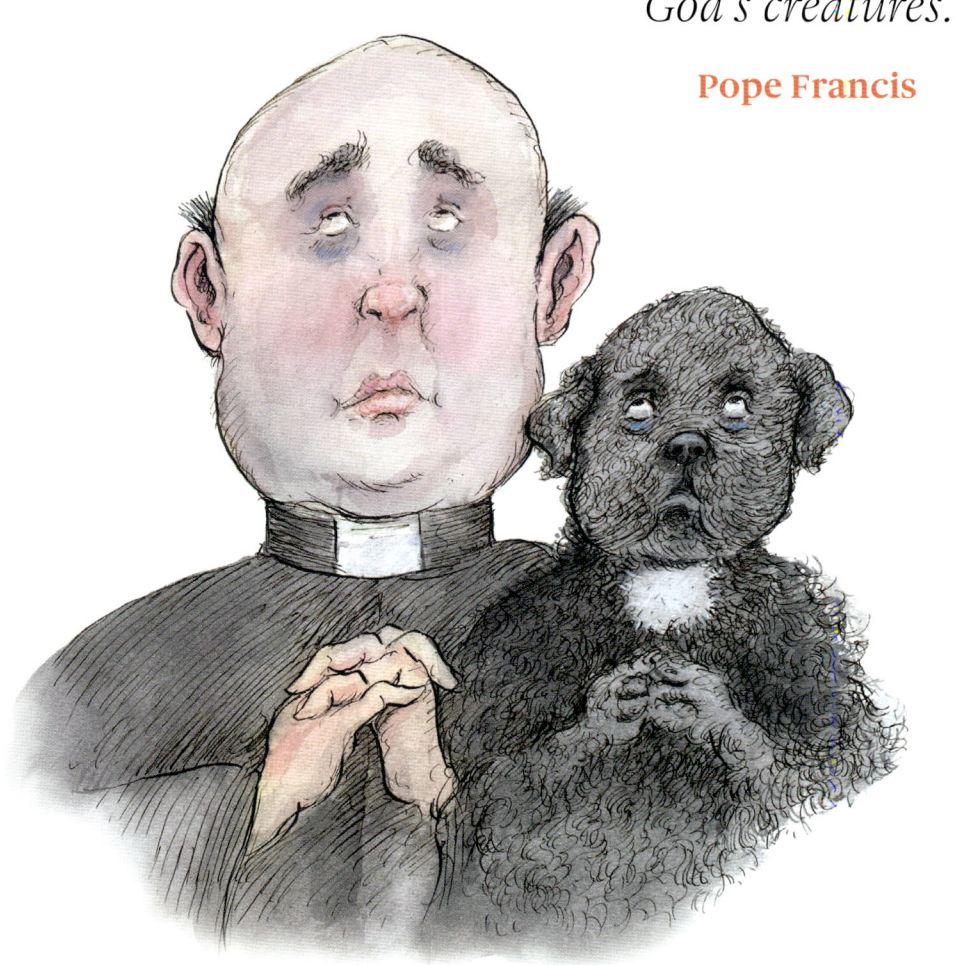

"*Paradise is open to all of God's creatures.*"

Pope Francis

"There's no such thing as a bad dog, just a bad owner."

John Grogan

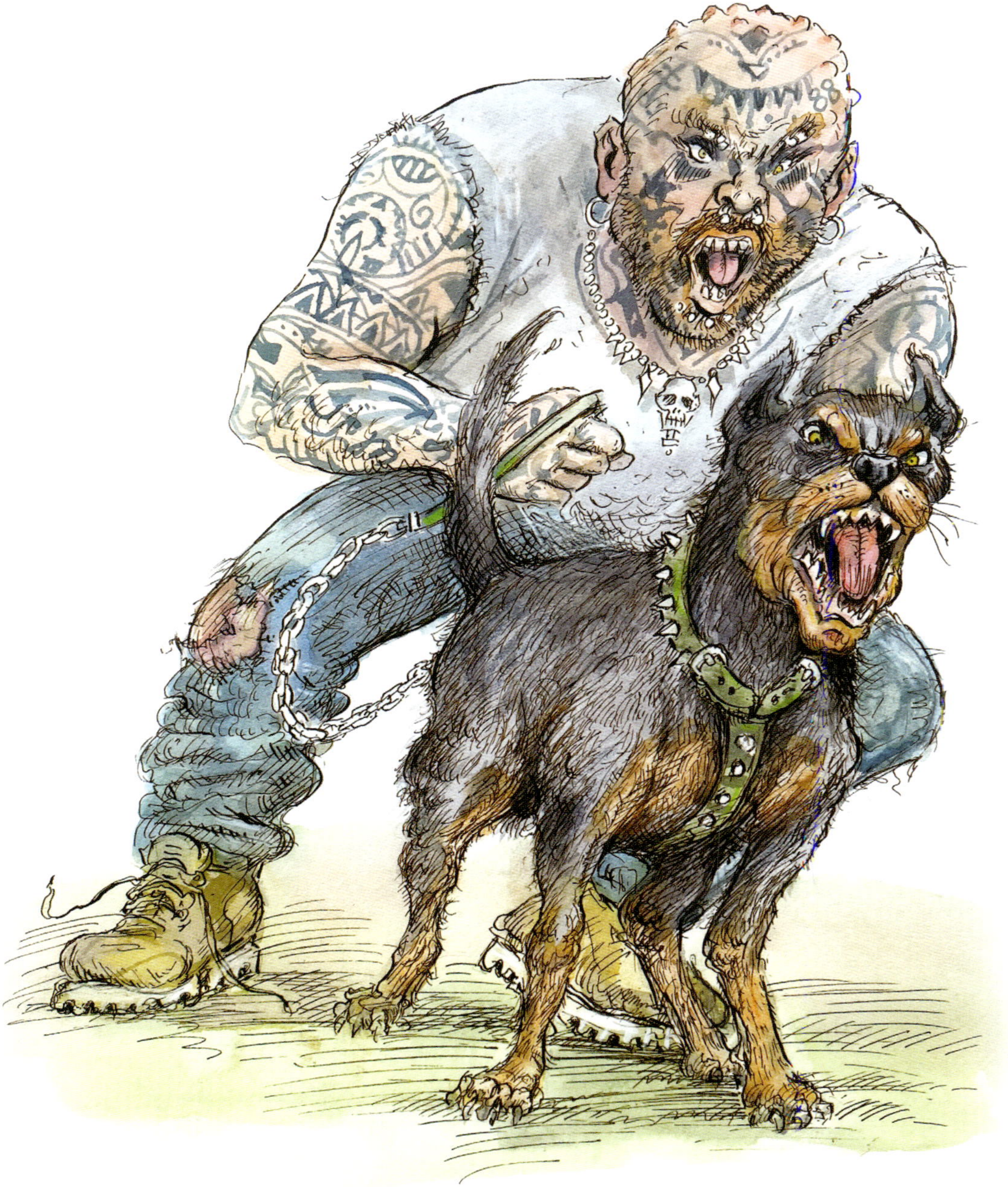

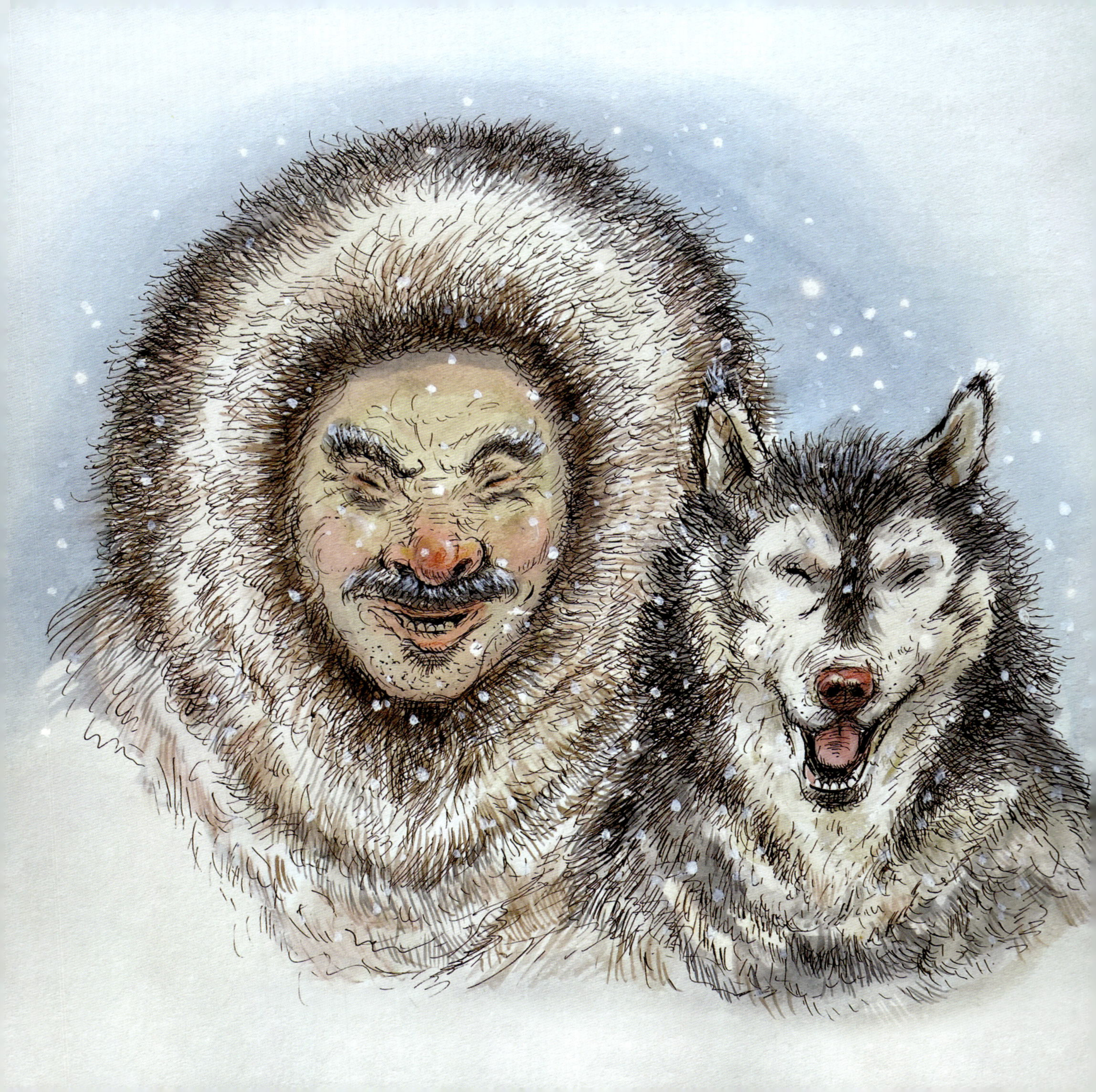

"Huskies have fifty words for snow."

Old Inuit saying

"Oh, I never got over those blue eyes."

Johnny Cash

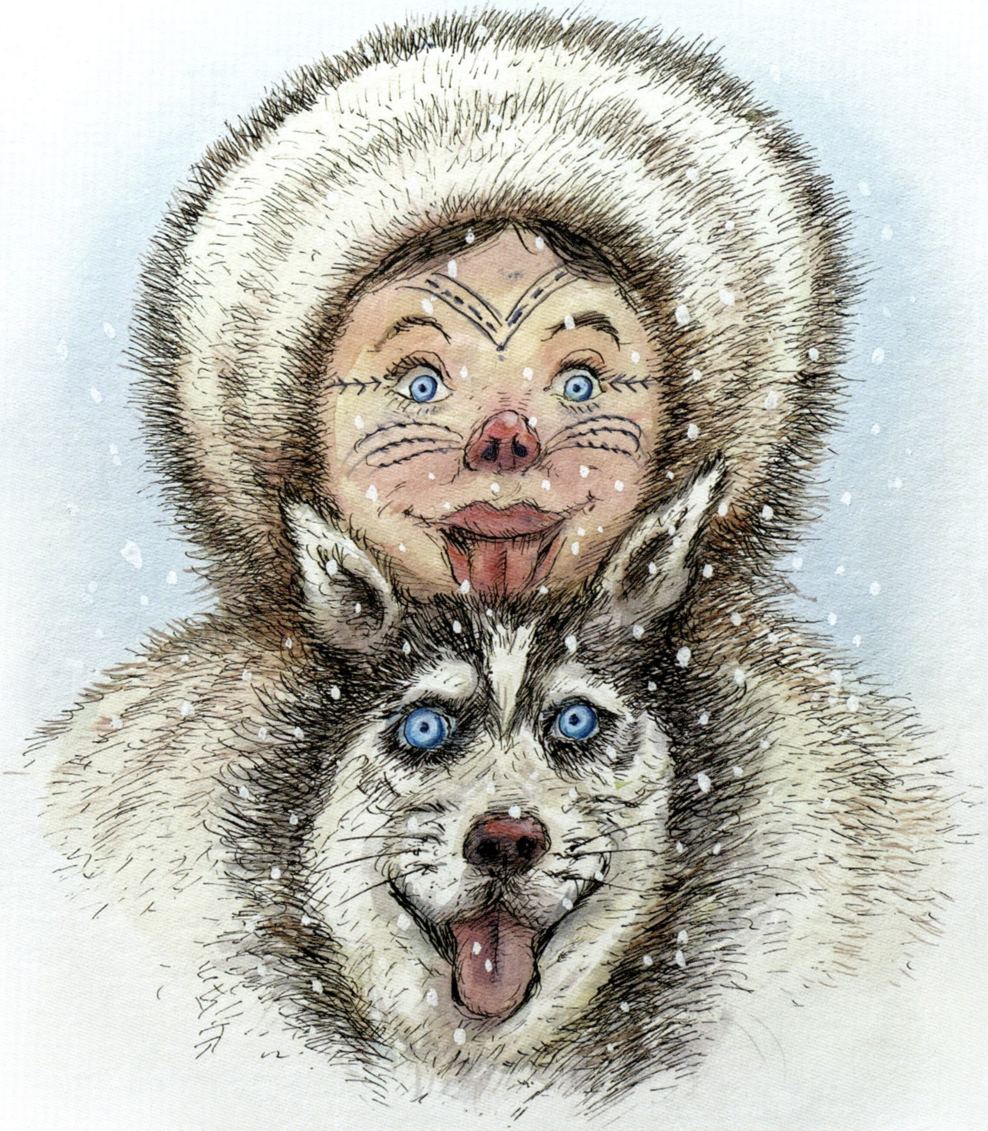

"Handle every stressful situation like a dog. If you can't eat it or play with it, then pee on it and walk away."

Anon

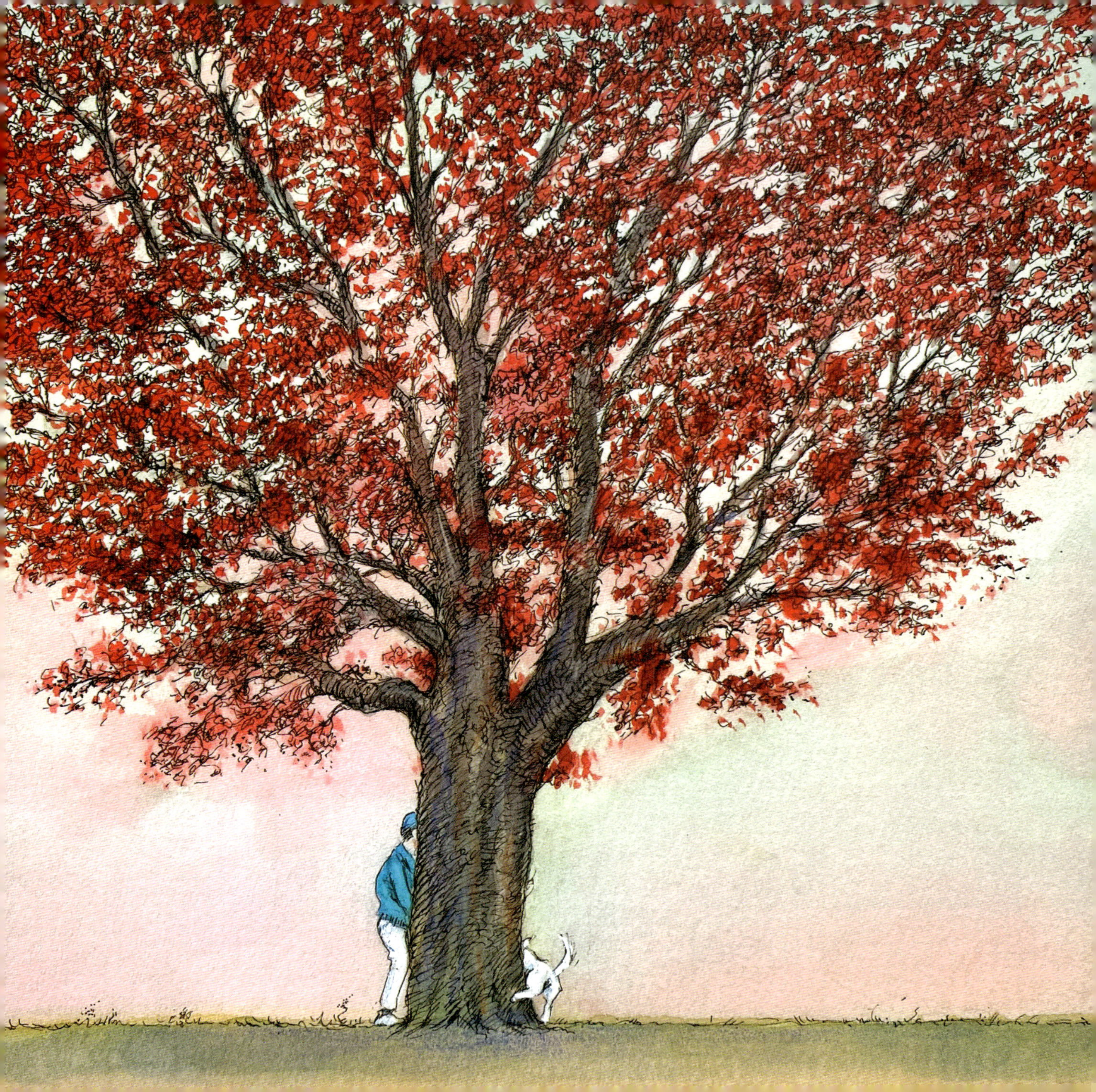

"The great pleasure of a dog is that you may make a fool of yourself with him, and not only will he not scold you, but he will make a fool of himself too."

Samuel Butler

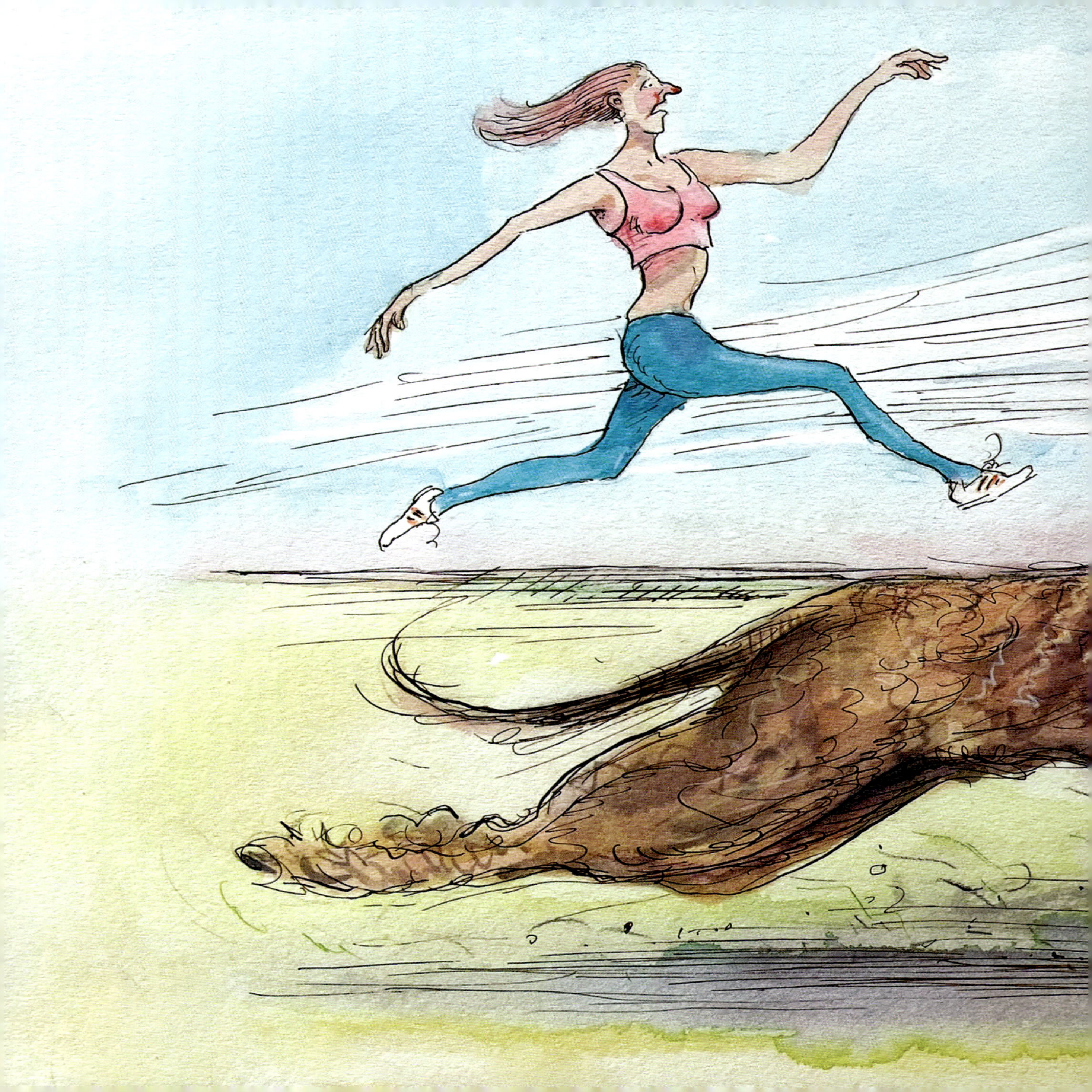

*"In order to really enjoy a dog,
one doesn't merely try to train him
to be semi-human. The point of it
is to open oneself to the possibility of
becoming partly a dog."*

Edward Hoagland

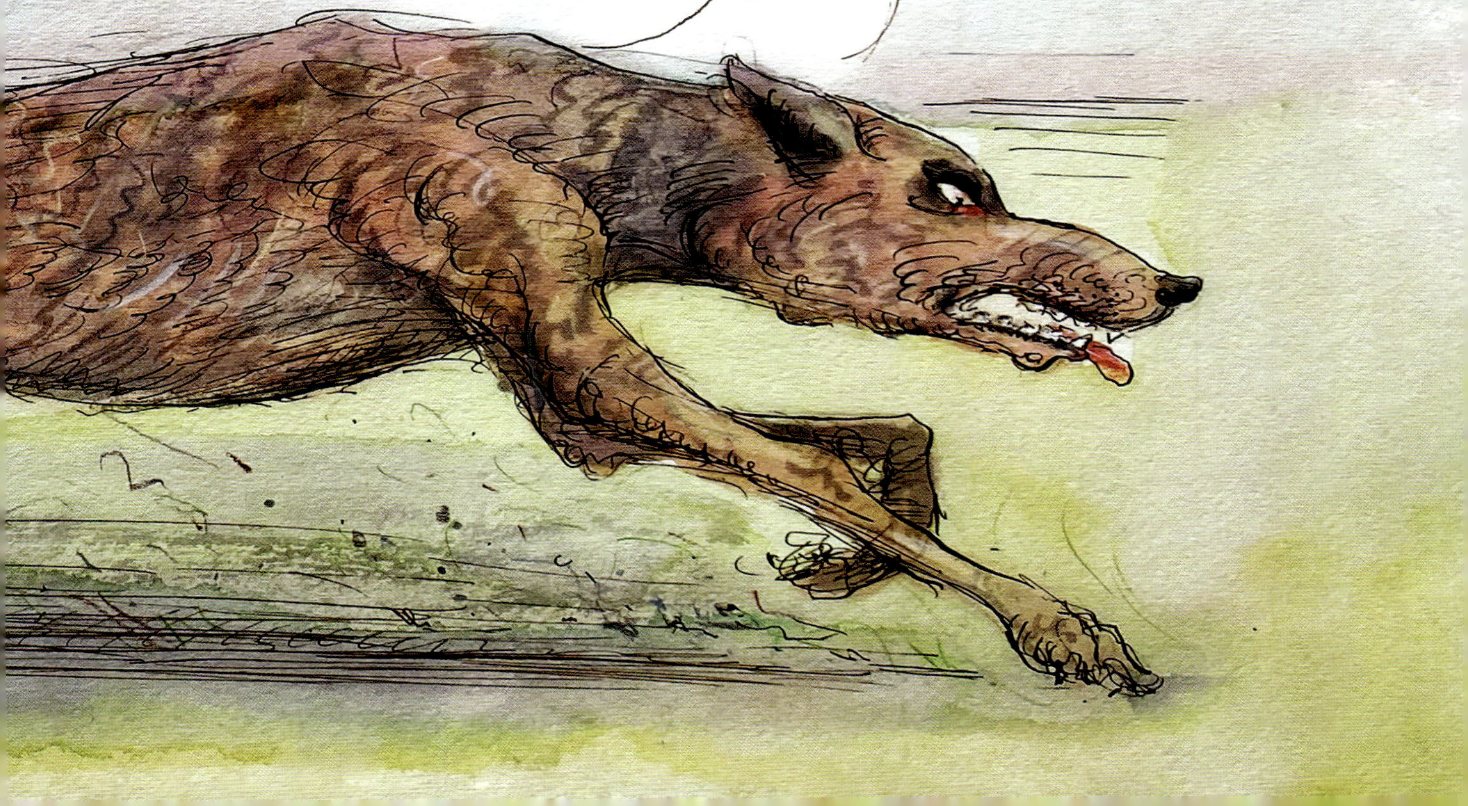

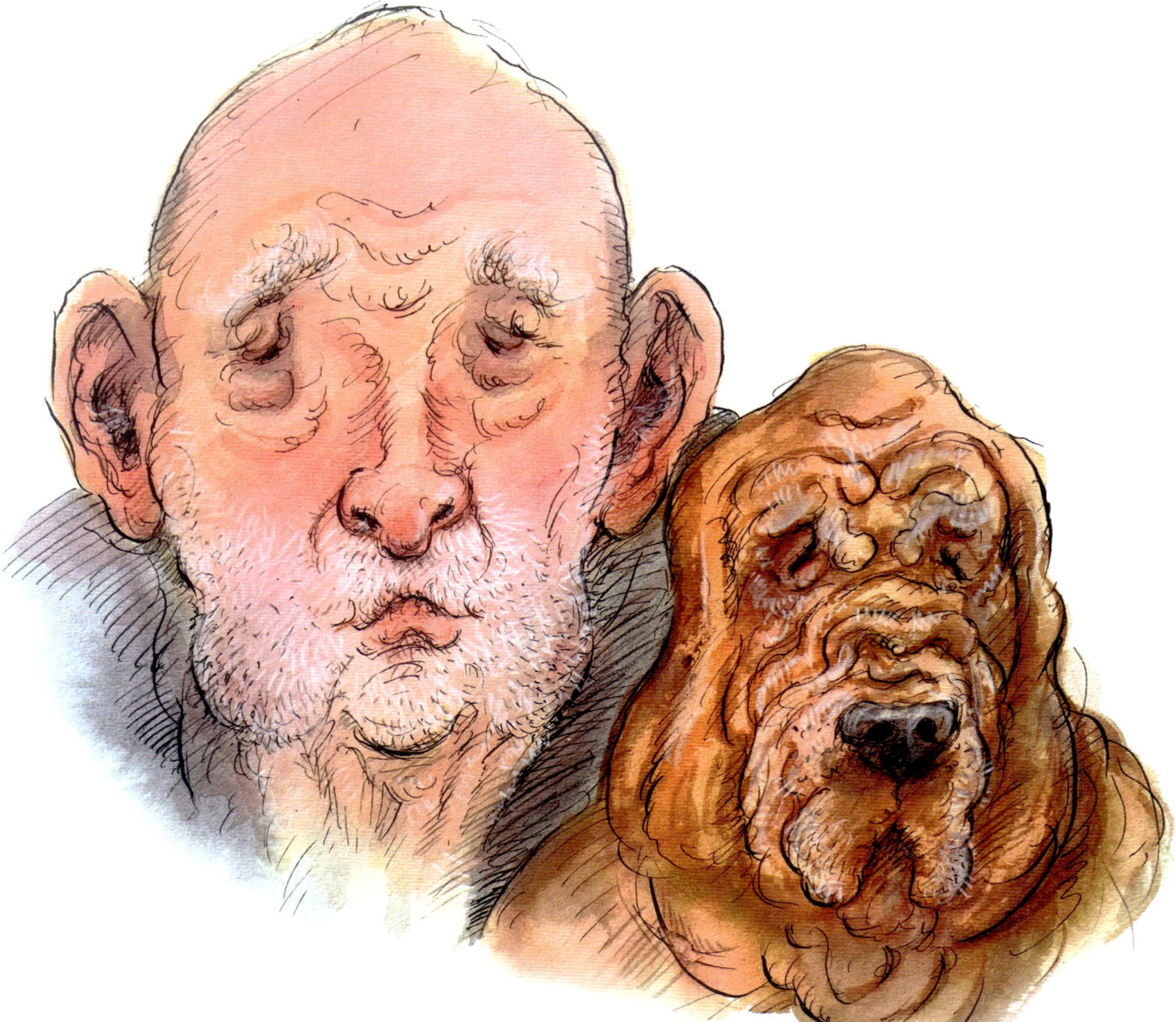

"There's only one thing worse than getting old … not getting old."

Anon

"When there are dogs and music, people have a good time."

Emmylou Harris

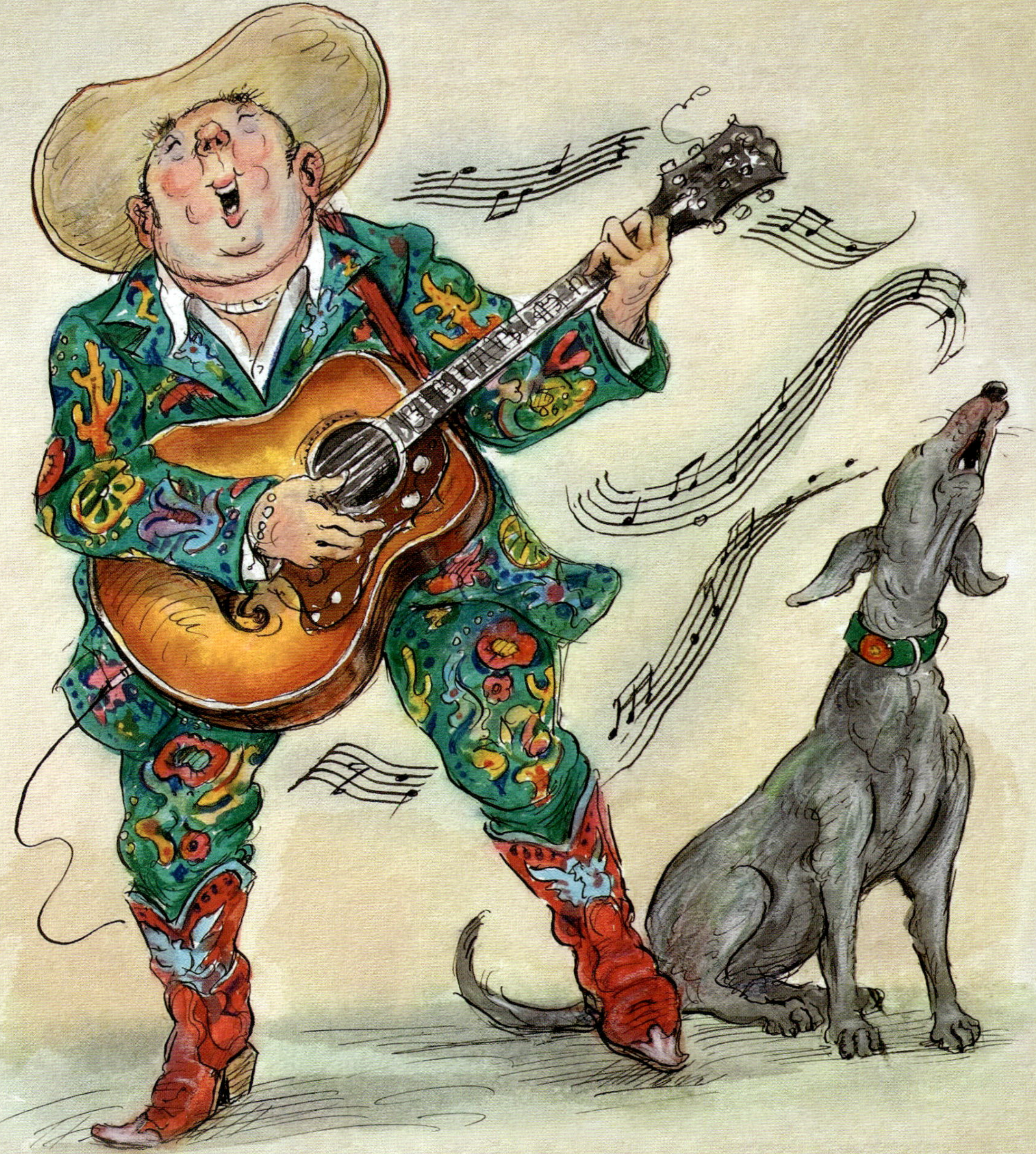

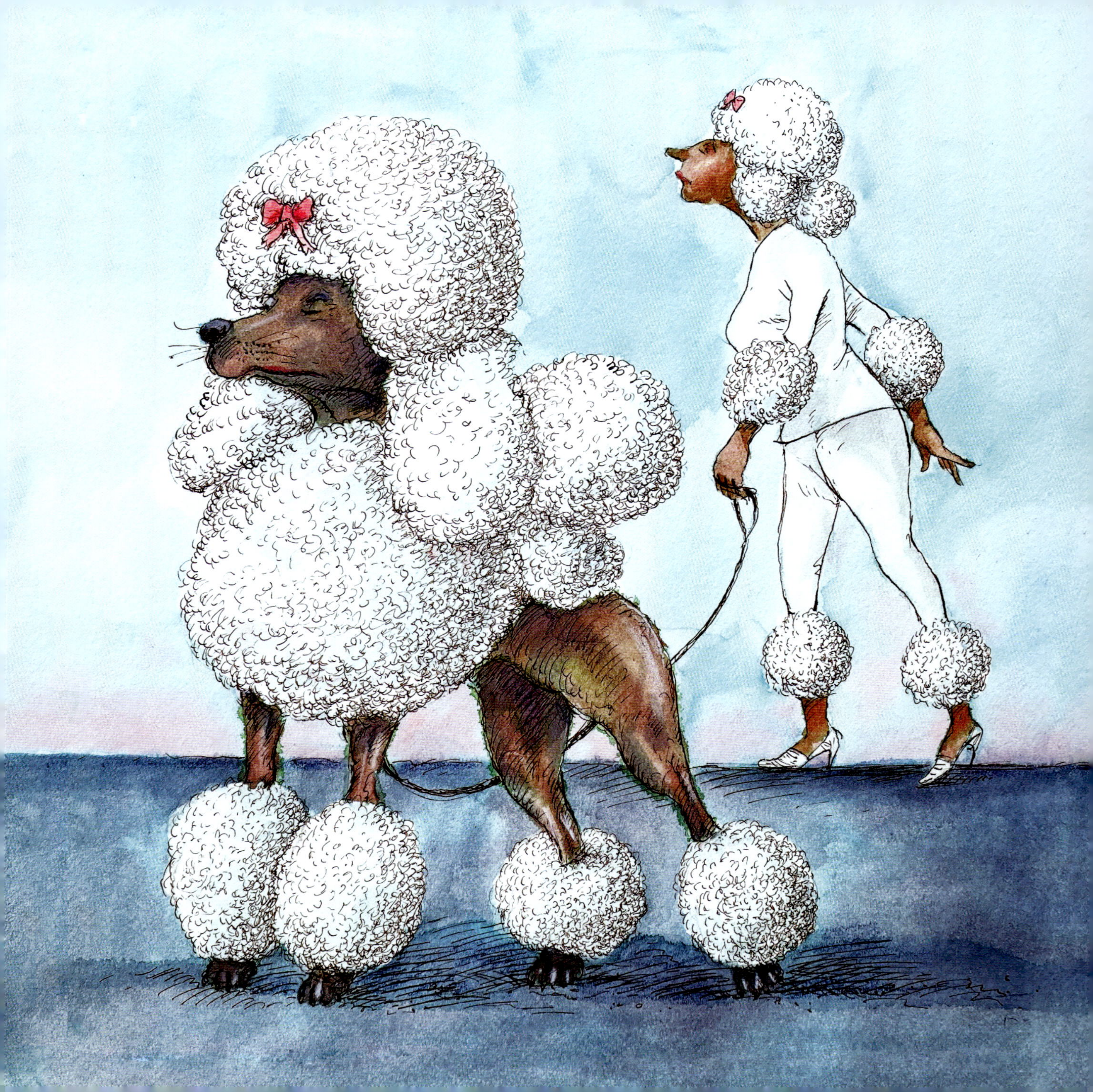

"There's nothing so similar to one poodle dog as another poodle dog, and that goes for women, too."

Pablo Picasso

"I don't care how you kill the little beasts, just do it, and do it now!"

Cruella de Vil

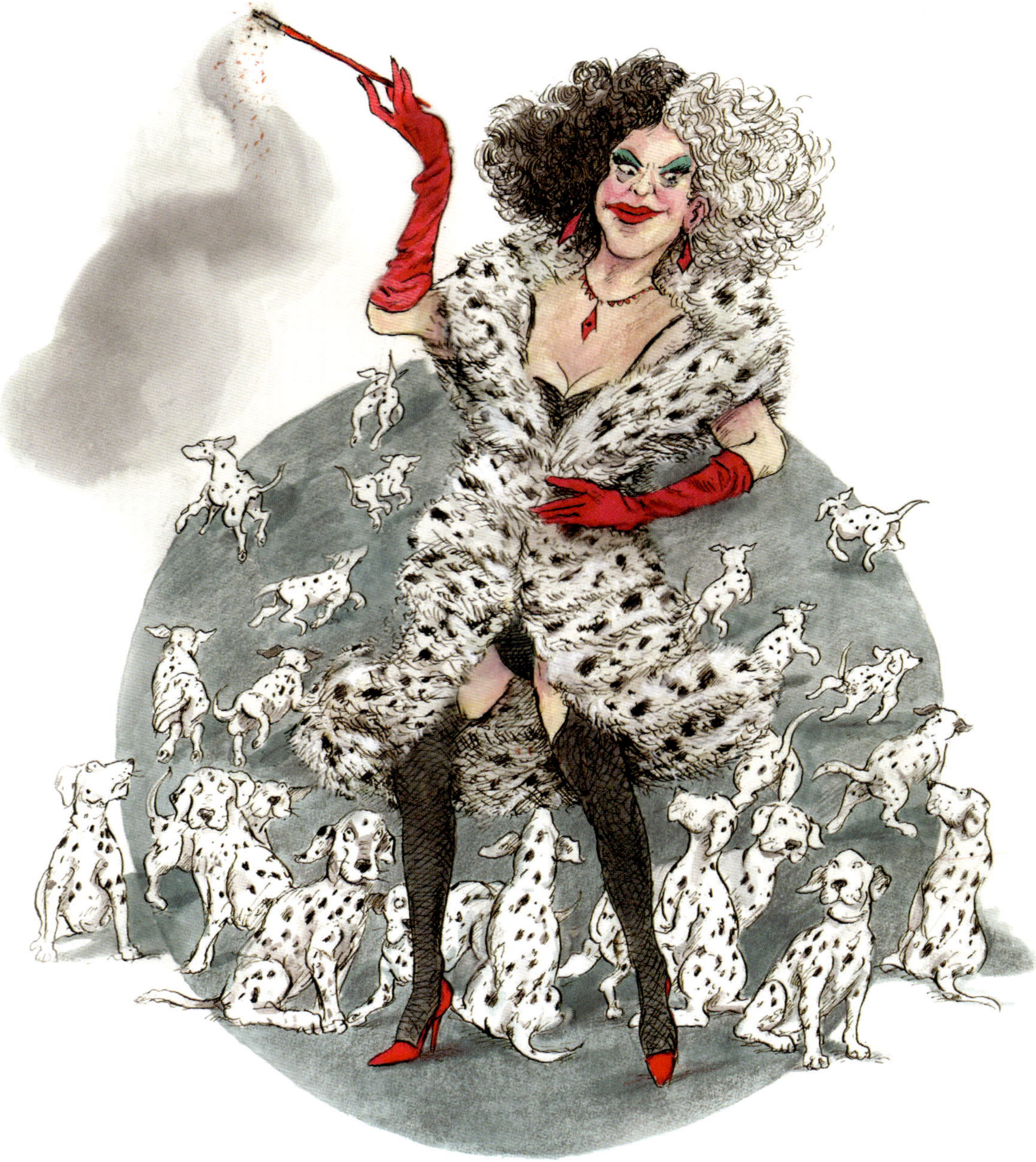

"If at first you don't succeed, swear a lot and give up."

Anon

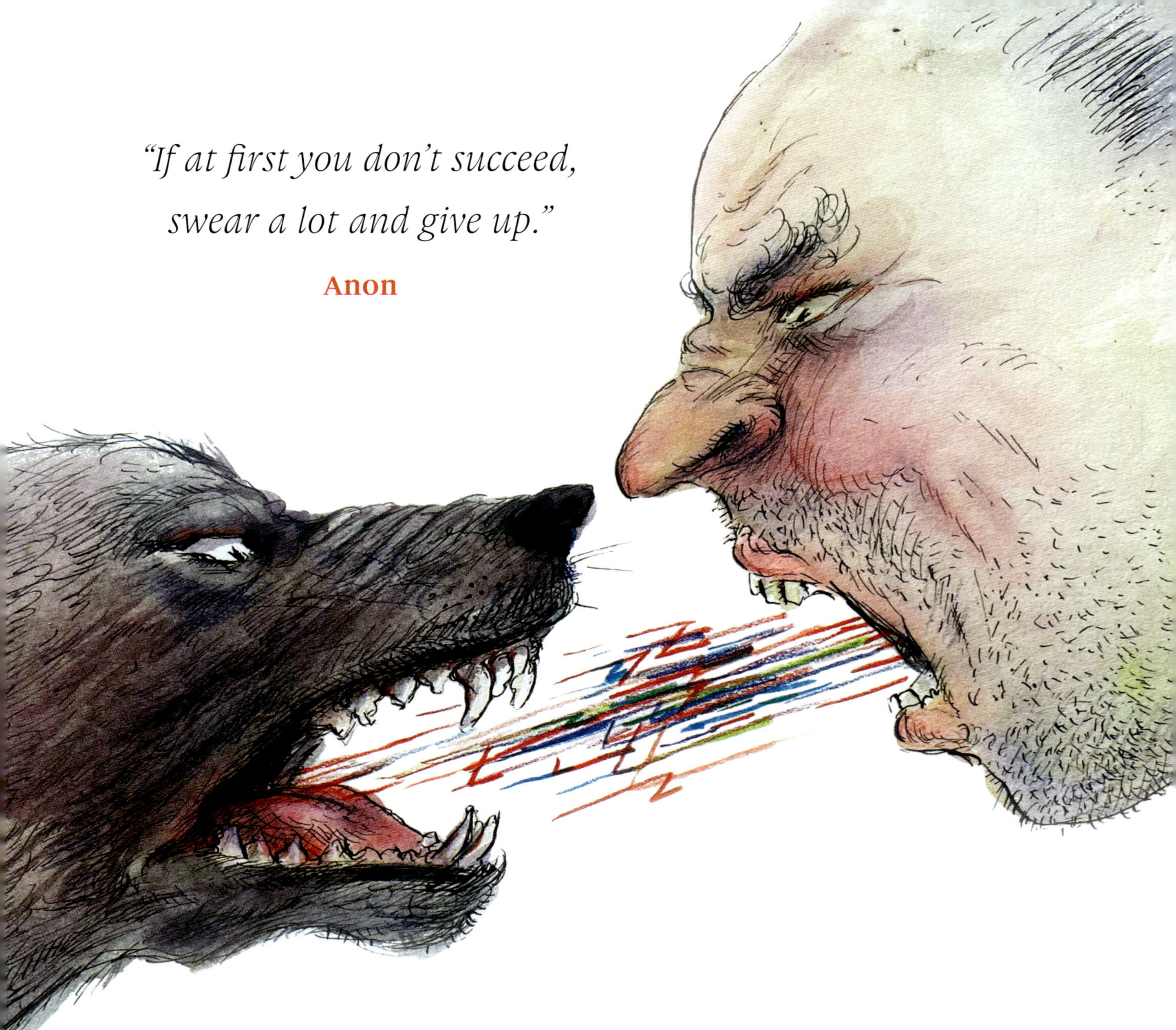

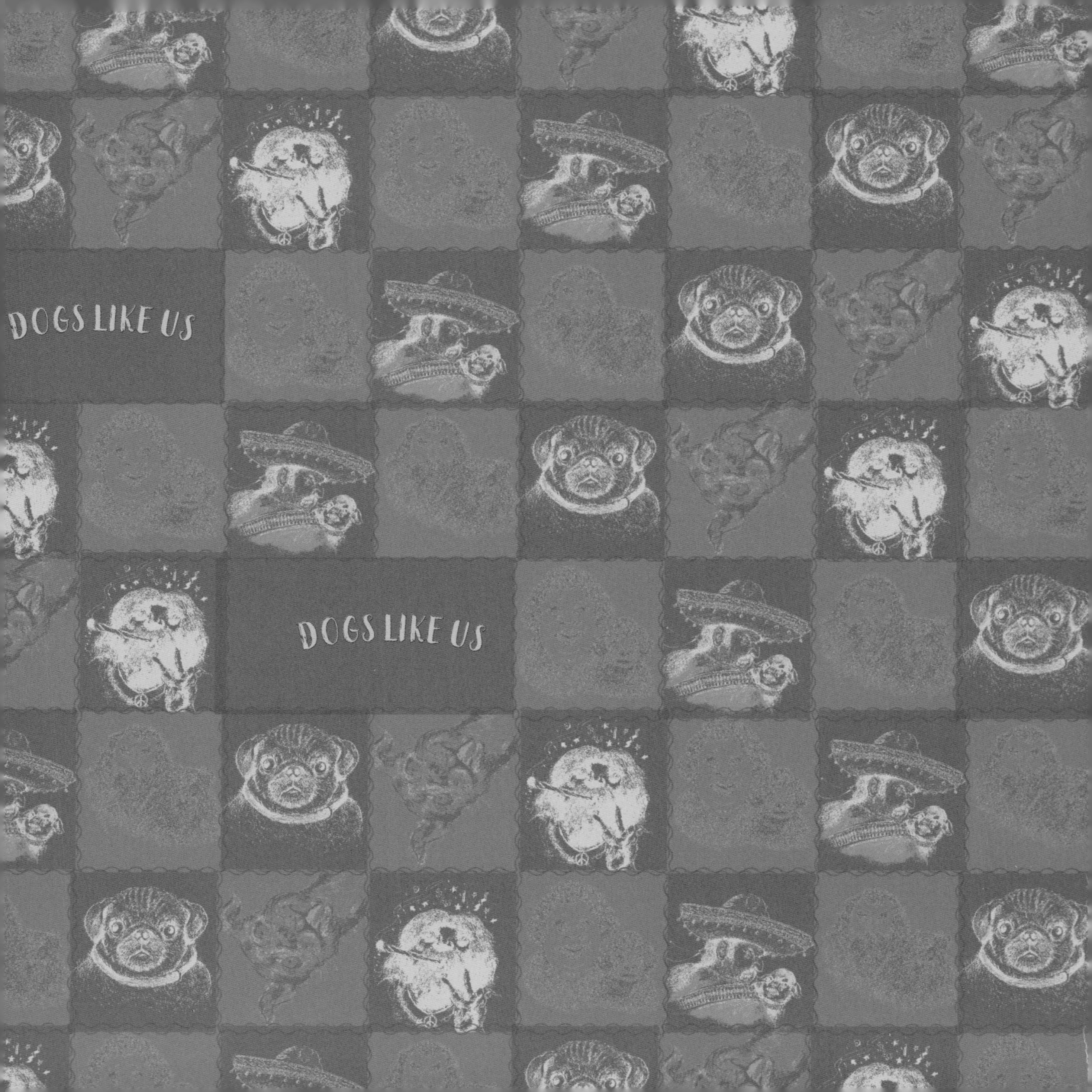
DOGS LIKE US
DOGS LIKE US